Protected Class Status for

Veterans in College

Douglas J. Herrmann

Emeritus Professor, Indiana State University

Bert Allen

Emeritus Professor, Milligan College

Copyright © 2012 Douglas Herrmann

ISBN-13: 978-1481063500
ISBN-10: 1481063502
To order additional copies, please contact us.
CreateSpace
www.CreateSpace.com
1-866-308-6235
orders@CreateSpace.com

iii

Dedication

This book is dedicated to all who have served, especially those who have made the ultimate sacrifice, and those who returned with medical problems that continued after their discharge. Along with other Americans, we are grateful to them for their service.

This book is also dedicated to all veterans who have wanted a college degree but have not obtained one because abuse prevented them from getting assistance from college educators.

Furthermore, this book is dedicated to all educators [professors, college administrators, staff] who recognize, respect, appreciate, and assist veterans in obtaining a college degree. Our gratitude is owed to these educators for taking care of past and present members of our military, thereby ensuring that our nation will remain safe and prosper.

iv

Acknowledgements

We thank educators and non-veteran students who support veterans as they seek a college degree. We are very grateful to Roland B. Wilson who first called our attention to the need of veterans for protected class status. We also are very grateful to Admiral John E. Gordon for leading the **Steering Committee** dedicated to establishing **Protected Class Status for Veterans** and to the members of this committee who have worked on this project for the past two years: Michael Dakduk, Ted Daywalt, Jeremy Glasstetter, Doug Gibbens, John Mikelson, Leslie Miller, Roger Peterman, Doug Raybeck, John Schupp, Michael Tomsey, Ron Trewyn, and Jer Yates.

We are grateful as well to colleagues who have also worked greatly to establish protection for veterans from abuse in higher education. These colleagues include the Officers and members of the **College Educators for Veterans Higher Education**, especially John Mikelson, Bill Smith, Leslie Miller, Julia O'Dell, Carol Yoder, Lynn Malley, Rita Johnson, Steve Fiore, Lewis Nelson, Roger Peterman, Charles Figley, Doug Franklin and the Leaders of **Operation Diploma:** Shelley MacDermid and Stacie Hitt. The several speakers [in particular Steve Kime, Kathy Snead, and Jer Yates] and the many attendees of the conference at the **Servicemembers Opportunity Colleges** in 2009 considered ways of **Improving College Education of Veterans.** We very much appreciate colleagues who have given valuable advice about the writing of this book and it's the contents, John Candelaria, Mike Caress, Jessica Saunders, Charles Hopkins, Roland Wilson, and especially David Vancil. We appreciate as well the many colleagues who could also be listed here because they also have worked to help veterans get college degrees.

Preface

Presently, our Veterans need help in obtaining college degrees. The new GI Bill will assist them with the financial costs of college. However, some veterans need help coping with abuse they receive from some professors, college administrators, and students, - abuse that the vast majority of non-veteran students will not encounter. (Staff members in most colleges invariably treat veterans with respect).

Who Might Benefit From This Book

The purpose of this book is to further inform American society and the higher education community about the abuse of some veterans by some professors and college administrators. This book reviews facts about such abuse and proposes that our nation needs to direct higher educators to cease engaging in this abuse and give veterans a better chance of getting a college degree.

The content of this book should be informative also to members of the federal and state governments who are responsible for drafting laws that may protect veterans from the abuse of professors and administrators in higher education. The book also may be useful to State Certifying Officials and Program Administrators who seek to help veterans obtain a college degree. Additionally, because of this book, veterans themselves may become more aware of the obstacles they are up against while they try to get a college education.

The two introductory chapters describe the legal requirements for protected classes in general and how veterans might merit a classification as a protected class. The third chapter reviews literature that report the abuse encountered by veterans in higher education. The fourth chapter describes how particular schools may be identified as abusive to veterans. The fifth chapter explains how some professors and college administrators came to abuse veterans. The sixth chapter proposes actions that may be taken to eliminate the abuse of veterans by college educators. The an epilogue for the book is presented in the seventh chapter. The eighth chapter presents a bibliography of sources relevant to information covered in the preceding chapters.

About the Authors

Herrmann and Allen became acquainted over the phone in 1992 when they were both outraged by a Newsweek article about research by MIT professors (Barnett and colleagues) that purportedly demonstrated the Vietnam War was fought mostly by the upper class. They requested from the professor a copy of the data on which the Newsweek article was based. Allen and Herrmann's analyses of these data showed that the statistics behind the Newsweek article were flawed and that the Vietnam War was clearly fought by America's lower class. Along with a VA psychologist, Steve Giles, Allen and Herrmann reported their findings in the Sociological Spectrum. Subsequently this journal awarded Allen, Herrmann and Giles a prize for the excellence of their article. Subsequently, Herrmann and Allen continued to stay in touch over the phone and email, and to write about the educational problems of veterans. Because of difficulties in the distance needed for travel, Herrmann and Allen did not meet face to face for the first time until 2007.

Along with several colleagues, Herrmann and Allen have spent much of the past several years investigating the discrimination and abuse of veterans by educators in American colleges and universities. Several colleagues at other institutions have shared with Herrmann and Allen their observations of the abuse of veterans by professors and administrators. These colleagues have also shared with them also shared with them what has been done to help veterans at their schools.

The authors' understanding of veteran abuse in college arises from long and dedicated careers of teaching at four higher educational institutions and from their experience serving in the military. In addition to the present book, Herrmann and Allen participated in, or contributed to, the writing of four books about the abuse of veterans in higher education in collaboration with two other educators (R. B. Wilson; C. Hopkins) very familiar with the abuse of veterans in American higher education.

Herrmann's Background for this book. Doug Herrmann's career in higher education included extensive publications on cognition, awards for teaching, and leadership positions as department chair at two institutions. In the middle of his career, he conducted survey research for the federal government. He retired from teaching in college in 2005.

Herrmann's experience in the military included the following. He enlisted in the Navy Reserve after high school and served in the Navy Reserve for a year. Subsequently he attended the US Naval Academy, from which he graduated in 1964. After graduation, he served in the Marine Corps, including service in Da Nang, Viet Nam (from the spring of 1966 to early 1967). He received the Navy Commendation medal, with a V insignia, for his service in Viet Nam. He was retired as a Captain from the Marine Corps in 1969. Beginning in 1975, he and his wife, Donna, have assisted Vietnamese immigrants settle in the United States.

Since the 1980s, he has done extensive volunteer work at VA hospitals. He began working in 1993 in veterans organizations that try to eliminate the problems of veterans in higher education. Since 2006 he has served as education liaison for the Indiana Employer Support of the Guard and Reserve.

viii

Allen's Background for this book. For more than 35 years, Bert Allen taught psychology and counseled students at Milligan College in Milligan Tennessee. Throughout his teaching career he served as a mentor for students, including veterans. He retired from college teaching in 2012.

Bert Allen's understanding of veteran abuse arises from his career of teaching and counseling at Milligan College. In addition to counseling veterans in college, he also volunteers to counsel veterans at a Veterans Hospital near to Milligan. His experience of counseling veterans made him very aware of the kinds of problems that are unique to veterans in college. He shared his observations of veterans' problems with Herrmann and colleagues at other institutions. Allen spent much of the past several years investigating ways to stop the discrimination and abuse of veterans by educators in American higher education.

Allen's understanding of veteran abuse also arises from his two years of service as a Specialist in the US Army. Like Herrmann, Allen served in Vietnam. Allen was an artilleryman; first as a member of a howitzer crew. While firing on January 10, 1969, Allen and three others were wounded by an incoming mortar round that exploded in their howitzer's parapet. Following that incident, he directed fire missions from the Fire Direction Center. Allen received the Purple Heart, a Bronze Star and an Army Commendation Medal for his Vietnam service. His understanding of veterans problems in higher educational institutions also comes from his participation in veterans organizations. For more than twenty years, Allen has been a member of Veterans for Peace and the Veterans of Foreign Wars.

ix

Table of Contents

Dedication   iii

Acknowledgements   iv

Preface   v

Chapter 1 - Protected Classes in Higher Education   **1**

Chapter 2 - Evaluating Whether Veterans Should be Given Protected Class Status   **9**

Chapter 3 - Evidence of Abuse of Veterans in in Higher Education   **15**

Chapter 4 - Assessing Abuse of Veterans at a Particular School   **29**

Chapter 5 - Why Some College Educators Abuse Student-Veterans   **41**

Chapter 6 - Preventing the Abuse of Student-Veterans   **49**

Chapter 7 - Epilogue   **77**

Chapter 8 - Bibliography   **79**

End of the Bibliography   *104*

Note: The term "veterans" in this book also refers to service members when not specified.

"The willingness with which our young people are likely to serve in any war, no matter how justified, shall be directly proportional to how they perceive the veterans of earlier wars were treated and appreciated by their nation."

George Washington

Chapter 1

Protected Classes In Higher Education

This can be a difficult world. Unfortunately, even in today' society, some people still discriminate against others on the basis of personal characteristics, ethnicity, religion, sex, gender, sexual orientation or other social differences. This discrimination comes frequently in the form of abuse. Generally, abuse can prevent individuals who are its targets from achieving their American dream.

The abuse of those discriminated against can come in several forms. The abuse can consist of negative things that someone says to a person, making the person appear inadequate to other people. Sometimes the abuse interferes what a person wants to do. Sometimes the abuse prevents a person from obtaining adequate medical care. Sometimes the abuse interferes with a person's efforts to get a college education. This latter form of discrimination is what this book is about, especially when the targets of the discrimination are veterans.

Abuse involves cruel maltreatment of a person. Abuse is harmful, wrong, unjust and immoral. (Abuse contrasts with damaging, incorrect, or neglectful mistreatment or with just a lack of knowledge on the offender's part). Whatever the form of abuse, it is never justified. At times, abuse may skirt the letter of the law, but regardless, it is wrong and when possible should be made illegal.

The focus of this book is on forms of abuse that prevent military veterans from obtaining a college-level or comparable education. This book also focuses on the most appropriate remedy for such abuse. It is argued here that military personnel, whether on active duty or honorably discharged, deserve protected-class status because of the special nature of their service to our nation. Appropriate protections of law will guarantee veterans the pursuit of their education beyond high school.

It is the view of some individuals that the military in our time is highly respected and that existing legislation is adequate to protect members of the military. However, particularly in higher education, such protection is not always the case. While the military is frequently viewed more favorably in colleges than in the Vietnam era, there is no guarantee that a positive view of the military will continue presently or in future generations.

In many colleges, administrative and faculty guarantees of protection of veterans that could be set by policy have not been set in place. Consequently, many colleges do not have policies that ensure veteran students will receive the same treatment already provided to members of the protected classes. And, sad as it is to consider, some cases of abuse of veterans (involving neglect, indifference, or overt negative behaviors) occur on some of our campuses and in some of our college classrooms.

Sometimes abuse is based on prejudice. Abuse can involve punishing a person when it is not justified. Regardless of its manifestation, abuse of any student is wrong. It is particularly heinous in the case where it is directed at an individual who has been subjected to the rule of military law and regulation in the service of his or her country. This abuse is not unlike groups of individuals (e.g., due to religious preference, race, sex, gender, or sexual orientation) who have been relegated to being targets of prejudice due to factors outside their control. As is the case, these groups have already received the protection against abuse by existing legislation. It is the view of many people that veterans should receive such protections.

Kinds of Legal Protection from Prejudicial Acts. Laws that prohibit abuse based on prejudice are said to "protect" the members of the group from such abuse. These laws include:

(1) The 1964 civil rights act.   This act outlaws major forms of discrimination on the basis of race, color, ethnicity, national origin, religious minorities and women. It helped end unequal application of voter registration requirements and racial segregation in schools, in the workplace and by facilities that serve the general public. Subsequent extensions of the 1964 civil rights act include
        (a)   Abuse on the basis of religion
        (b)   Abuse on the basis of sex
        (c)   Abuse on the basis of sexual orientation
(2) Age Discrimination Act of 1975. This law prohibits discrimination based on age in programs or activities that receive federal financial assistance, such as, financial assistance to schools and colleges provided by the U.S. Department of Education.
(3) Americans with Disabilities Act of 1990. This law was enacted by the U.S. Congress in 1990 and later amended with changes effective January 1, 2009. This is a wide-ranging civil rights law that prohibits, under certain circumstances, discrimination based on disability.
(4) Title IX. This is part of the Education Amendments of 1972 that states no person in the United States shall be denied on the basis of sex, either the benefits of, or subjected, to discrimination under any education program or activity receiving federal financial assistance.

When Do People Need Protection?

One reason for protection under the law is to ensure that people who apply for a job are evaluated fairly. Similarly

Similarly the performance of employees should also be evaluated fairly. The same is true for people who apply for admission to a college or university. Admission of students to college should be fair for all applicants. Similarly the academic performance of students should also be evaluated fairly on the basis of their schoolwork. Unfortunately both college admission and evaluation of academic performance is not always fair.

When is Discrimination Illegal? A biased assessment will result in discrimination because of incorrect information. Such discrimination in hiring and evaluation of job performance is illegal if it disadvantages a group that is supposed to be protected by law. Similarly, biases in college admission or evaluation of academic performance are illegal if they disadvantage a group that is supposed to be protected by law. However, such biases are not necessarily illegal for groups not protected by law.

Protected Class

"Protected Class" is a term used in United States anti-discrimination law to describe groups of people who are legally protected from discrimination. If individuals or employers discriminate against a member of a protected class, they may be punished as dictated by the law (from fines to incarceration to loss of accreditation). As mentioned above, certain groups are considered "Protected Classes" wherein members of these groups are disliked and even hated, referred to pejoratively, and described primarily by: their race or color, national origin, religion, sex, gender, or sexual orientation. The hate for a protected class has typically been captured in a term that refers to the prejudice involved: for example, racism, ethnic bias (spics, kikes), religious bias (Catholicism, Protestantism, Judaism, Islam), sexist or gender bias (male, female), or sexual orientation (straight, homosexual, bi-sexual).

The promise to not discriminate against protected classes pertains: to any kind of employment discrimination, to hiring, and to job performance. In the case of employment matters, protected class programs are sometimes referred to as involving "affirmative action." These programs are responsible for maintaining "equal employment opportunity" (EEO).

Abuse That Warrants
Protected Class Status

However, discrimination in employment is not the only issue concerning protected classes. The primary issue is that members of a particular class are abused because of discrimination. Consider the abuse experienced by current protected classes.

In American history, before they were given legal protection, members of a protected class could be denied employment simply for being a member of these classes. Additionally, people were free to verbally abuse members of the now protected classes, including false criticism that constitutes libel and slander. It was not uncommon to refer to such a person with a prejudicial term associated with the nature of their class, such as: nigger, spic, kike, whore, and straight, homosexual, bi-sexual. Abuse was also facilitated because the targets of abusers were easy to identify visually, because: of the color of their skin, kinds of clothing (such as worn by a nationality, a religion, males and females), postures and ways of talking characteristic of members of a group (racial national, males and females, and sexual orientation).

In addition to being verbally abused, before being given protection, these classes also were the targets of administrative abuse. Obtaining licenses for driving or for construction were complicated or nearly impossible whereas obtaining licenses for those the majority of people was not difficult. Sexual harassment was frequently encountered.

In addition to being verbally abused and administratively abused, before being given protection, members of these classes were the targets of inadequate medical care. It was difficult to get medical care from clinics run by doctors belonging to the major class.

For the purpose of this book, discrimination against service members includes current members of our armed forces and discrimination against veterans includes those discharged from the military. Like members of some protected classes, veterans are very easy to identify visually when in uniform. They are often easy to identify visually when not in uniform because of their military posture.

Abuse by Passive Observers

Some college educators (professors and administrators) allegedly abuse some veterans while they study for a college degree. It is difficult to estimate how many college educators engage in abusive practices. Some veterans who are educators believe these practices occur sometime at many colleges and universities. Currently such abuse is legal.

It should be noted that many educators recognize, respect and appreciate veterans in their classrooms. Many veterans and service members do not experience any abuse. However, it is held that some educators hold negative beliefs about veterans, that they are killers and are stupid. Like racism, sexism and other classes that are prejudiced against, those who dislike or hate veterans can be said to hold beliefs against veterans (a belief in "veteran-ism" – that veterans are inferior in a variety ways).

Passive Observers. Nevertheless, educators not involved in abuse, but who have knowledge of it, still present a problem for veterans and service members. Those not involved in abuse but are aware when it occurs are guilty of the "bystander effect." Unfortunately, bystanders facilitate the bad practices of those engaging in abuse.

Educators involved in abuse often take strength from bystanders who confer approval on abuse by remaining silent about the abuse that is conducted. When observers do not openly object to the discriminative and abusive behavior of their colleagues, bystanders make things worse for veterans. This is similar to what happened prior to the civil rights era when some citizens said nothing while African Americans were socially mistreated, physically abused and even murdered by groups prejudiced against them. Every protected class has suffered more than they would have if bystanders had chosen to not ignore the abuse they observed, to stand up against discrimination and the abuse that goes along with it.

Shared Responsibility

Many academics have observed colleagues discriminating against, and abusing, veterans and service members. On such occasions, some bystanders may have disapproved of such abuse and attempted to get the abuse stop his or her maltreatment of veterans. On other occasions, some bystanders actually disapproved of such abuse but said nothing about it to the abuser. Their inaction of abusers may unwittingly increase the likelihood of subsequent occurrence of these abusive practices. Moreover, when the effects of bystanders are taken into account, along with that of abusers, it would appear that nearly all-higher educators have contributed in some fashion (indirectly or directly) to the abuse of veterans and service members.

The effects of discrimination and abuse have led some veterans and service members either to not apply for college or to drop out of college because the added pressure of abuse made it difficult for them to keep up with their studies. Alternatively, those who continued in college, even in the face of abusive practices, had their academic performance negatively affected. Certainly, some veterans and service members succeed in college despite discrimination and abuse. However, those veterans and service members who do well in college are fewer than should be the case.

Discrimination and Abuse of Class Members After they are made a Protected Class

Once established as a protected class, discrimination and abuse of class members decreases substantially. The press, politicians and educators became careful to not say something negative sabout members of the classes of race or color, national origin, religion, sex, and minority sexual preferences. Similarly, violent hate crimes are reported as occurring much less often to members of classes currently protected by the law.

All of the established protected classes are protected from being abused while they seek a college degree. Some higher educational institutions explicitly respect protected classes in their policies. Stated or not, abuse of protected class members can lead to punishment (such as a fine, loss of employment or possibly loss of accreditation). (Note: Chapter 1 of the Bibliography presents literature on protected class status in general).

Chapter 2

Evaluating Whether Veterans Should Have Protected Class Status

The major issue in awarding protected class status is whether members of this class are at risk for discrimination and abuse because they belong to this class. The purpose of this book is to evaluate the claim that student veterans are currently the targets of discrimination and various types of abuse: verbal abuse (libel, slander, fraud); administrative abuse (inferior teaching, inadequate financial aid, and other unfair treatment such as biased grievance procedures); and inadequate health care at some college health centers.

Veterans Are Not a Protected Class in Higher Education

Higher education makes it a matter of policy to protect members of legally established classes (groups of minority races, national origin, certain religions, sex and gender, or minority sexual orientation) in employment and educational matters. Alternatively, veterans have protected class status in employment issues of colleges and universities but the educational process is not protected for them while veterans seek a degree in college.

This chapter explains how student veterans do not qualify for protected class status in higher education. The fundamental matter to consider is whether or not it can be shown that professors and administrators sometimes abuse veterans.   (The term 'veteran' in this book refers to individuals who either have been discharged from military service, individuals who are presently on active duty, or individuals who serve in the National Guard, or in the Reserve). Some people are members of protected classes by virtue of accidents of birth, over which they have no control or reason to reject (such as race and nationality). Similarly some veterans are born into families that have a strong culture to serve in the military; also some families have a long lineage of military service, a lineage that some believe is genetic.

While receiving protection for employment issues, because of the lack of protection for educational matters, veterans are not called a protected class. Also as a result of this lack of protection, members of the academic community (college professors, administrators, staff, and non-veteran students) are free to treat student-veterans in a discriminatory manner, should they desire.

Below are some examples of mistreatment of veterans in some colleges and universities. These examples are provided to familiarize you with some complaints of veterans. It will be up to you to decide whether these examples deserve further consideration. Chapter 3 discusses these and other examples of veteran abuse to provide you with additional information about such abuse.

Verbal Abuse of Student Veterans in College

Some veterans have experienced discrimination and abuse while attending college in various forms, including unfair treatment: in class, in the grading of papers. Indeed, there has been a wide range of verbal abuse and unequal treatment in and outside of the classroom. This unfair treatment of veterans includes the following.

(1) Veterans might be treated differently than non-veterans in tutoring or testing.
(2) Expression of slanderous negative attitudes about student veterans.

    (3) Incorrect teaching practices that take away time
         that student veterans need for studying.

    (4) Negative teaching practices that hinder the learning
         of veterans.

Administrative Abuse of Student Veterans in College

Professors and administrators should be taught how to recognize student-veterans as accurately as they recognize non-veterans. Professors and administrators should also be instructed to teach veterans in the same manner as they teach non-veterans.

    (1) provide the same opportunities to student veterans for financial aid as provided to non-veteran students.

    (2) ensure that veterans are assisted in their job search at graduation with the same effort given to assisting in job search for non-veterans.

    (3) provide grievance procedures for veterans that are just as fair as the grievance procedures given to non-veterans.

Medical Abuse of Student Veterans in College

Some student veterans suffer from a lack of needed medical care in college. The reasons for the lack of appropriate care are straightforward. The staffs of college health centers rarely have the training necessary to treat all of the illnesses, disorders, or disabilities that veterans sometimes bring to college. Additionally, there are no legal requirements for health centers to provide good medical care for veterans whereas as the health centers are legally required to provide sound medical care for members of the established protected classes. As a result:

(1) Some student veterans receive inadequate medical care for routine medical problems at their college.

(2) Some student veterans receive inadequate medical care for service-connected disabilities at their college.

(3) Some student veterans are not referred properly for their health problems to non-VA facilities or to local VA facilities.

Should Veterans be Given Protected Class Status?

Such status would be needed if veterans are verbally abused, administratively abused, or medically abused more than non-veterans and more than members of other protected classes. The issue is not whether veterans are not treated differently when this should occur. Veterans are supposed to be treated differently than other groups of students for academic services such as financial aid, transfer credits, housing, and job placement on graduation. Nevertheless there are no administrative practices at some institutions to ensure that veterans are treated in the ways that are expected for them.

Some academics deny that they or any of their colleagues engage in any discrimination or verbal abuse of student veterans. Some publishers also claim that none of their authors who are professors or college administrators discriminate against or verbally abuse student veterans. In subsequent chapters, you, the reader, can investigate further the allegation that veterans are abused in college and decide whether or not such abuse occurs.

Chapter 3 examines abuse in detail from different media.

Chapter 4 proposes how a particular college or university may be discovered to abuse student veterans.

Chapter 5 addresses why professors and college administrators verbally and administratively abuse student veterans.

Chapter 6 proposes what might be done to discourage professors and college administrators, short of protected class status, from verbally and administratively abusing veterans. This chapter proposes how protected class status for veterans might be established.

An epilogue addresses some issues common to the six chapters The bibliographies for each of the preceding chapters are presented in an eighth chapter. (Sources for the first chapter, on **Whether Veterans Should have Protected Class Status,** are also presented in the Bibliography).

Summary

While they receive protection for employment issues, veterans are not called a protected class. As a result of this lack of protection, members of the academic community (college professors, administrators, staff, and non-veteran students) sometimes feel free to treat student-veterans in a discriminatory manner. The next chapter will examine in detail whether veterans are abused in higher education.

Chapter 3

Evidence of Abuse of Student Veterans

Veterans should be made a protected class if evidence clearly demonstrates that some professors and/or some administrators abuse some veterans. This chapter has the purpose of presenting such evidence as reported in the media (books, magazine articles, journal articles, web articles, videos, power point files, word processing files, surveys). These media attest to the abuse of college students with a military background (service members of the regular military branches, members of the Guard, and Reservists) by some professors and college administrators. The abuse addressed in these publications pertains either to verbal abuse, administrative abuse, or medical abuse.

There are no data that indicate exactly how many veterans are abused in college. Nevertheless, there is ample survey research that indicates many veterans encounter one or more of the three kinds of abuse. However, it should be noted that many veterans do not encounter abuse. Similarly, many professors and/or many administrators do not abuse any veterans. Regardless of the amount of abuse and the number of educators engaging in abuse, no veteran deserves any abuse.

The prevalence of abuse of service members was recognized by Defense Department (DoD) in the mid 1970s. Because of the abuse that had been recognized, DoD formed an organization called Service members Opportunity Colleges (SOC) that was intended to promote better treatment of service members who attended colleges and universities. Higher educational institutions were invited to join SOC if they promised to not mistreat service members.

Later SOC members were also asked to not mistreat veterans. Presently more than 1800 colleges (out of the nearly 4000 American higher educational institutions) belong to SOC and participate in SOC programs. The creation of SOC demonstrates that the Department of Defense recognized service members and veterans were encountering abuse by at some higher educational institutions and that action needed to be taken to discourage this abuse.

This chapter presents three sections wherein each section addresses one of three kinds of veteran abuse (verbal abuse; administrative abuse, and medical abuse) by a professor or college administrator. Some examples of the kind of abuse are presented in each section. Verbal abuse consists inappropriate and rude statements to veterans. This kind of abuse consists of incorrect and deliberately false statements to veterans. Administrative abuse consists of incorrect procedures or the failure to provide procedures that should be provided to veterans. Medical abuse consists of incorrect treatment or the failure to provide correct medical treatment to veterans.

At the end of each section about a kind of abuse, the kinds of abuse of other protected classes by a professor and/ or college administrator is described. After information is presented in the three sections about abuse of veterans, the chapter briefly reviews the kinds of media sources that provide the information about the three types of abuse of veterans.

Verbal Abuse of Veterans

Sometimes things are said to veterans that are not true. Some colleges provide veterans with incorrect information to convince them to enroll there. For example, admission officers often tell veterans they would get lots of financial aid and scholarships after enrollment. However, the aid is not always provided later. The admission officers of some schools ask veterans to sign a contract that obligates them to get all of their education at the school, rendering them financially indebted to the school for their entire education.

In addition, some admission officers tell veterans that all of their credits approved by military would be transferred to the school after enrollment. However, later the veterans do not receive these credits. Some schools also promise veterans that they will receive transfer credit for courses taken at other colleges; later none of the credits for these courses is transferred

Some professors at some schools are known to openly make false negative statements in class about military service. Non-veterans almost never report hearing professors saying slanderous things to them. In that non-veteran students are aware of which other students in a class are veterans, anti-military comments of professors isolate the veterans in a class and ostracize them. Such isolation of veterans interferes with their performance in class and makes interaction outside of class with non-veteran students difficult. One professor referred to negative stereotypes of veterans in some exam questions, making the student-veterans uncomfortable when they took the exam.

Some schools fail to help student-veterans with acquiring academic skills as promised. Student-veterans are sometimes told they will receive academic assistance in their courses whenever it is needed. Later they discover such assistance is not available. Student veterans may be falsely told that they will follow educational programs that have been tailored to their interests. However, some schools do not live up to this promise by ignoring a veteran's military occupational specialty (MOS) when advising veterans on what courses to take.

Verbal Abuse Encountered by Protected classes

Members of the protected classes (race and color, national origin, religion, sex (or gender), sexual orientation) rarely encounter fraud in college because such treatment of protected class members is clearly discriminatory and illegal. Professors and college administrators almost never verbally abuse members of the currently established protected classes such as race, color, religion, females or males, and members with minority sexual orientation because academics know they will be punished legally for violating protected class laws.

Administrative Abuse of Veterans

Failure to Provide Services. Veterans are supposed to be given certain services not provided to non-veterans. For example, these services may pertain to teaching, financial aid, employment, and to a grievance process. Some college administrators knowingly do not provide these services. In other cases, veterans are supposed to be given the same services as non-veterans. Unfortunately the services rendered to veterans are often inferior to how the services are provided to non-veterans.

Practices for Teaching Student-Veterans in College. Some veterans report that professors devote less time to teaching student veterans than to teaching non-veteran students. At some schools professors fail to give students academic help once they know these students are veterans. Such abusive teaching practices lead student veterans to fail to understand course content and to spend more time than necessary to learn the correct course content. Some professors penalize veterans who may miss class due to injuries, illnesses or disabilities caused by their military service. These educators also penalize Guard members for missing class in order to attend drills.

Some student-veterans report that they are sometimes given incomplete or inaccurate advice by professors and administrators about courses, a major, and/or a minor. Some colleges will assign a low grade for courses taken at the time of deployment without allowing the Guard member or Reservist to take an incomplete in these courses. These practices make it more difficult for a veteran than a non-veteran to obtain a college degree.

Professors and administrators need to be taught how to recognize student-veterans as accurately as they recognize members of protected classes (because of visual cues, posture, and speech habits). Professors and administrators should assist veterans in certain situations. For example, veterans suffer excessive social, economic, and educational discrimination as a result of taking themselves out of the fabric of civilian life to serve in the military. Also veterans suffer significant social deprivation at some colleges for holding pro-military and patriotic beliefs.

Financial Aid Problems. Some schools fail to provide veterans with appropriate financial-aid procedures and information. The financial aid offices at schools provide little or no financial aid to recently discharged veterans, whereas these offices do offer aid to other special interest groups, protected classes and even international students. Many schools have scholarships for certain non-veteran student groups but do not have scholarships tailored to the background of veterans. Most schools do not attempt to create any. Also many colleges do not provide assistance to veterans in finding financial support for a veteran who has a family.

Employment Problems for Veterans at Graduation. Some schools fail to give veterans all of the help they need for finding a job after graduation. Career center counselors often are not familiar with resources to help veterans find jobs (such as employers who are veterans, and military-related web sites, including Military Connection, Military Exits, and Military Job Zone). Career centers tell student veterans that they will be given as much help as non-veterans with finding post-graduation employment. In actuality, veterans are often not given such help.

Grievance Procedures. Some administrators or professors ignore the needs of veterans for college services. When this occurs a veteran can file a grievance. Unfortunately, when a veteran files a grievance, it generally is unsuccessful more often than the grievances of non-veteran students. Difficulty with grievance complaints often appears to be due to grievance panels not including any veterans on the panel.

Administrative Abuse Encountered by Protected Classes

Members of the protected classes (race and color, national origin, religion, sex (or gender), sexual orientation) rarely encounter administrative problems in college because such treatment of protected class members is clearly discriminatory and illegal. Professors and college administrators almost never abuse members of the currently established protected classes because academics know they will be punished for violating protected class laws.

Medical Abuse of Student-Veterans

Colleges are obligated to treat the medical problems of all students who have college health insurance. When possible, they will also treat students without health insurance or they will refer these students to a medical facility that can treat them. Colleges sometimes provide poor health care to veterans because, first, veterans often do not purchase health insurance because they feel their health needs will be taken care of by the VA. However, obtaining VA medical care can be difficult if the VA Hospital is distant from a veteran's school. This problem is not due to an inadequacy of the college or university except that higher educational institutions should inform veterans about how far the VA hospital or clinic is from their school and why it is due to their advantage to buy the college's health insurance.

Even if student veterans have health insurance, most staff of most health centers have not been trained to treat or refer many of the medical conditions (physical and psychiatric) of veterans. Consequently colleges sometimes provide poor health care to veterans, second, because of the lack of staff training about the medical needs of veterans.

Student veterans who do not have health insurance need referrals to go elsewhere for health care. Veterans sometimes get inadequate health care in college because, third, the clinics or hospitals that veterans are referred to are often unable to treat the health problems of veterans. While the VA medical facilities are generally known to be outstanding, what is not well known is that VA Centers vary in their capability to treat different kinds of wounds, illness, and disorders. Because the variation in this capability is not well known, college health centers may unknowingly refer veterans to VA facilities that are not prepared to treat certain veterans medical problems.

Many non-VA facilities are not prepared to treat the medical problems of veterans. Although it may seem that the VA is responsible to treat all medical problems of veterans, the responsibility always begins with the staff of a college's health service that should know how to refer a veteran elsewhere for care.

Colleges provide poor health care to veterans, fourth, because there are no laws that make poor treatment of veterans illegal. Whereas poor medical treatment of members of protected   classes can be judged a crime, poor treatment is not   illegal   when it comes to veterans who seek care in college health centers. Some professors are also aware that student veterans miss class due to poor health more often than nonveterans.

Even if health center staff is prepared to treat and refer veterans properly, a school may not know how to equip its campus to assist disabled veterans.   Many colleges and universities sometimes appear oblivious of the disabilities that veterans experience because of using inappropriate campus-wide practices to assist veterans with these disabilities. Customary changes in sidewalks and railings are not enough. Many veterans have disabilities that require special equipment and assistance in order for them to succeed in college.   For example, some veterans are super sensitive to sounds and lights. These veterans can be equipped with devices that lessen this sensitivity. Also, some veterans are unable to take notes and need assistance to do so in class.

Similarly professors often are uninformed of a veteran's disabilities and unaware of how to teach people with certain disabilities. Nevertheless, a professor should be informed when a disabled veteran is in class and should be instructed on how the veteran can be assisted in this course. Professors and administrators should be also learn the common symptoms of Post-Traumatic Stress Disorders (PTSD) and transient brain injury (TBI), and to alert the College Health Service if a veteran needs assistance with PTSD or TBI, or other health problems.

Medical Abuse Encountered by Protected Classes

Members of the protected classes (race and color, national origin, religion, sex (or gender), sexual orientation) rarely encounter medical abuse in college because such treatment of protected class members is clearly discriminatory and illegal. Professors and college administrators almost never medically abuse members of the currently established protected classes such as race, color, religion, females or males, and members with minority sexual orientation because academics know they will be punished for violating protected class laws.

Sources about the Abuse of Veterans in Higher Education

Information about the abuse of veterans in higher education can be obtained in several ways: books and articles (magazine, journals, or web; including videos, power point files, word processing files; and the results of surveys). The sources used to write this chapter are listed in the bibliography under chapter 3. Most of the abuse addressed in publications pertains to verbal and administrative abuse but several articles address medical abuse of college health centers. Fourteen articles report on surveys that demonstrate that veterans are abused in college.

Books that Report Abuse of Student Veterans

At least eleven books have been published in the past decade that are pertinent to verbal abuse, administrative abuse, and medical abuse of student veterans. The titles and authors of these books are provided below; the full citations of these books are listed in the bibliography. In some cases the books focus on current abuse of educators in higher education. In other cases the books focus on programs that may prevent abuse of veterans in higher education.

Most of these books provide scholarly references that document the origins of information about abuse of veterans. Readers who want to learn more about higher education abuse of veterans are invited to read one or more of these books.

Books that Address Abuse of
Veterans in College

Campus Kit for Colleges and Universities.
Powers, J. T. (2008a).
Campus Kit for Student Veterans. Powers, J. T.
(2008b).
Creating a Veteran Friendly Campus: Strategies for
Transition and Success New Directions for   Student
Services, Ackerman, R. & DiRamio, D. (Eds.)(2009).

Educating veterans in the 21st Century: Herrmann, D. J.,
Hopkins, C., Wilson, R. B. & Allen, B. (2009).
Improving the College Education of Veterans. Hopkins, C.,
Herrmann, D. J., Wilson, R. B., Allen, B., & Malley,
L. (Eds.) (2010).
Nature of the Higher Educational Programs forVeterans
(2010) Franklin, D.
Progress in Educating veterans in the 21st Century.
Herrmann, D. J., Hopkins, C., Wilson, R. B. &
Allen, B. (2011).
Veterans in Higher Education: When Johnny and Jane come
marching to Campus. DiRamio, D. & Jarvis, K.
(2011).
The Higher Education of Veterans. John Schupp (2011)
The Higher Education Landscape for student service
members and   veterans in Indiana. Sternberg, M.,
MacDermid Wadsworth, S., Vaughan, J., & Carlson,
R. (2009).
Veterans College Handbook. Wilson, R. B. & Herrmann, D.
(2012).

Articles About How Student Veterans
Cope with Abuse in College

In the past fifteen years many magazines, journals, web sites, and videos have called attention to the abuse of student veterans while they seek a college degree. The references for these articles are presented in this book's Bibliography, in section B. In all, the bibliography presents more than 100 articles on teaching abuse, administrative abuse, and medical abuse of student-veterans.

Below is a list of twelve articles that provide examples of the abuse of veterans. They are listed here by title; these titles indicate the nature of the abuse covered in the article. The complete references for these articles are listed in the bibliography. Readers are invited to examine some of these articles to get a feeling for specific cases of abuse facing veterans who return to college.

Articles about Higher Education's
Abuse of Veterans in College

1- "A serious breach of ethics committed by the faculty and administration of the Columbia University School of Social Work against an Iraq war veteran, Sergeant First Class (SFC), Ret. Eli Painted Crow." See Bhagwati, A. (2011), taken from McCaffrey's Facebook page. See also: anu@servicewomen.org "brad@lunamediagroup.com", "John DMikelson" <john-mikelson@uiowa.edu>

2- "Brian Teter Disabled vet kicked out of college. Iraqi war veteran claims discrimination." Brown, W. (2011) http://video.foxnews.com/v/1181448445001/disabled-vet-kicked-out-of-college/?playlist_id=86856 [Also in a movie, A Last ounce of courage]

3- "Clout-Less: How University of Illinois Changed Admissions Procedures to Keep Military Veterans Out." Chicago Tribune (2009) http://www.scribd.com/doc/17547381/Cloutless-U-of-I-Discriminates-Against-Veterans. May 9

4- "Military recruiters promise 'money for college', but recent veterans find that tuition benefits fall short." Farrell, E. F. (2005). Chronicle of Higher Education. May 13.

5- "College Is for Veterans, Too" Herrmann, D. J., Raybeck, D., & Wilson, R. (2008). " The Chronicle of Higher Education, November 21.

6- "Two urgent issues facing our community: 1) A threat to New GI Bill benefits 2) Some for-profit schools are exploiting loopholes in the federal law to make a buck." IAVA (2011) see IAVA web site.

7. "College forcing student out because she has service-related PTSD." Labedz Poll, M. (2009) University of Massachusetts.

8- "Half of Student Veterans Have Contemplated Suicide, Study Shows." Lipka, S. (2011). American Psychological Association, National Meeting. Washington, D.C.

9- "Anti-military sentiments persists on elite campus." Petrovic, K. (2006) Retrieved Jan 16, 2006 from https://www.vfw.org/inde.cfm?fa=news.magDt&dtl=1&mid=2766

10- "From combat to college: A tough transition that few understand." Steigmeyer, R. (2009, February 21) Wenatchee World. Retrieved from http://www.wenatcheeworld.com/article/20090221/NEWS04/702219970

11- "First battle: serve in military. Next battle: finish college." The Missourian. Wilkes-Edrington, L. (2007). Retrieved on September 14 2007 from http://www.columbiamissourian.com/stories/2007/05/26/first-battle-serve-military-net-battle-finish-col/

12 "Here's a college list we have faith in." Editorial – friendly and unfriendly colleges. Klimas, J. (2012). Navy Times, April 23.

Survey Research Articles
on Reports of Abuse of Veterans in College

Survey research about abuse of student veterans has grown over the past decade. For example, a recent survey conducted by the Iraq and Afghanistan Veterans of America indicates that abuse is directed at veterans of the current wars: IAVA (2012). Fifteen survey articles on veteran abuse are listed in the Bibliography under Chapter 3. Survey data confirm the conclusions drawn about abuse of veterans in the books and articles listed above and in the Bibliography.

Incorrect Interpretation of Veteran Responses by Some Survey Researchers

Some survey researchers concluded that veterans are socially less skilled than non-veteran students because veterans reported participating less than non-veterans in campus activities. However, this conclusion about a lack of social skills is simply false and a mistaken inference to draw from survey results. Veterans participate less in campus activities because some professors have led non-veterans to ostracize the veterans. Also veterans participate less because they are older, have families to care for, and have outgrown campus activities. Research staffs fail to recognize that their incorrect attitudes about student veterans persuade other academics and non-veteran students to be rude to student-veterans. Incorrect conclusions about surveys of veterans also mislead educators about how veterans may benefit from social interactions in college.

Survey Research about Abuse of Protected Classes

Survey research almost never direct questions about college to members of the protected classes (race and color, national origin, religion, sex (or gender), sexual orientation). Consequently, there are no data comparing reports of veterans with reports by members of protected classes. Nevertheless, it is possible to compare reports of abuse by veterans to comparable reports by non-veteran students that includes reports by members of protected classes. This research indicates that veterans report more abuse on surveys about college than non-veterans. Members of the protected classes (race and color, national origin, religion, sex (or gender), sexual orientation) would be expected to report little or no abuse on surveys about college because such treatment of protected class members is discriminatory and illegal.

Summary

If the reader is interested in whether veterans should be made a protected class, he or she is advised to read one or more of the books and articles listed above, and the other books and articles listed under Chapter 3 in the Bibliography.

The sheer number of sources reporting different examples of veteran abuse indicates that abuse of veterans actually occurs in some American colleges and universities. Moreover, survey research confirms what books and articles have reported about verbal, administrative, and medical abuse. This evidence of the three kinds of abuse of our veterans is appallingly shameful. Such poor treatment of our veterans warrants assigning legal protection to them in order to keep these abuses from continuing.

Chapter 4

Deciding Whether a Particular School Abuses Veterans

Some schools assert that they protect certain classes of citizens. Sometimes the classes they promise to protect include veterans. Alternatively, the classes protected by a college or university often does not include veterans.

A statement that service members and veterans have protected class status has legal impact should a school violate this status. A service member or veteran can sue a school if it fails to provide the protection promised. Below are some of the schools that have a policy to treat veterans as a protected class or to treat them without discrimination (this list is not exhaustive).

Louisiana State University
Ohio State University
University Alabama
University of Central Oklahoma
University of Colorado
University of Iowa
University of Kentucky
University of Massachusetts
University of Minnesota
University of Missouri
University of North Carolina
University of South Carolina
University of Utah

As mentioned previously, there are more than 3000 higher educational institutions in the U.S.; more than 1800 of these schools belong to an organization called Service Members Opportunity Colleges (SOC). Members of SOC are required to promise to provide some protection for service members and veterans. However, no system exists to determine whether a SOC school keeps this promise and no system of punishment is enforced for SOC schools that do not keep this promise.

Some colleges say they give veterans special treatment without specifying protected class status. Here are some of the schools that promise such treatment (this list is not exhaustive).

> Ball State University
> Dartmouth College
> George Mason University
> Indiana State University
> Indiana University Southeast
> Ivy Tech Bloomington
> Ivy Tech Sellersburg
> Ivy Tech Wabash Valley
> Purdue University
> University of Evansville

Assessing whether a school supports a protected class policy for veterans requires an evaluation of a school's policies and practices for verbal abuse, administrative abuse, or medical abuse. Practices of abuse of veterans employed at some colleges and universities are described below. More detailed descriptions of these practices were presented above in Chapter 3 and in the sources cited in the Bibliography for Chapter 3 and Chapter 4.

Kinds of Educational Abuse of Veterans. Most of the abuses that veterans encounter belong to the same categories of problems that non-veterans encounter. These problems include: selecting an appropriate college; making the transition to college life; acquiring the academic skills needed in college; adjusting to the culture of a college; interacting with professors, administrators, and other students; financing college; obtaining transfer credits; participating in college educational programs; maintaining one's health; providing for oneself and family; and finding employment on graduation. However, the abuses in these categories challenge veterans differently from how they challenge non-veteran students.

Before people became members of a protected class, some of these people were subjected to abuses that made making a transition to college difficult. Similarly, some veterans have not obtained a college education because they failed to make the transition from military to college life. Many veterans know veterans who do not recover from the emotional problems experienced in the military and combat. Many veterans also know other veterans who are highly intelligent and could have succeeded in college but these other veterans became homeless or ended up in prison. Some highly intelligent service members and veterans would have obtained a college degree had they not committed suicide. Many veterans could succeed in college if they were helped with making a transition to college.

Identifying a School as
having an Anti-Veteran Policy

If a reader wanted to determine whether a particular school employed policies or customs against veterans, determine whether the abuses in Chapter 3 and discussed below occur at the school.

Abusive Transition Practices

Professors, college administrators, certifying officials, college health center staff, members of the DOD, the VA, and veterans service organizations fail to help veterans make the transition of service members and veterans to college campus. They make the transition difficult by not explaining college programs, services and policies for veterans and military personnel. Some colleges do not brief professors and college administrators about how to anticipate the enrollment choices of returning veterans and military personnel and how to make a higher educational institution suitable for veterans. Some schools do not provide training in study skills that have been designed specifically for veterans.

Evaluation of a school's veteran abuse should include consideration of whether a practice is a result of poor management or deliberate abuse. Depending on the severity of abuse, schools can be classified as Veteran-Friendly or Veteran-Unfriendly. The veteran friendliness of a school is discussed later in this chapter after the review below of possible bad practices of schools.

Some schools allow non-veteran students on campus to be unfriendly toward veterans. Instead professors and administrators should teach non-veteran students that there is no good reason to be unfriendly and rude to service members and veterans. If a student objects to military action, he or she should be instructed to make their objection known to government officials responsible for such action.

Abusive Practices of College Educators

Abusive Practices by Academic Advisors. Some advisors provide a student-veteran with incorrect advice about courses that may be taken for a major, a minor, an elective, or general education requirements. Also, despite a school's promise to do so, a school may not provide education of the specialty that a student veteran wants.

Some schools have a reputation for not wanting the military or veterans on campus during and after the Vietnam War. Some of these schools do not tell prospective student veterans that it had anti-military or anti-veteran protesters on campus in the past. Some schools do not tell prospective student veterans that it has prohibited establishing a ROTC program at the school. These schools and other schools prohibited military recruiters from working on campus.

Prior to admission, some schools falsely promise to provide information about their programs, requirements, accreditation, and whether or not the school is based on profits from the education they provide. Sometimes college administrators fail to anticipate the enrollment choices of returning veterans and military personnel. As a result, certain courses are not available for some veterans to take.

Abusive Transfer Credit Practices

A school may fail to award to a student-veteran's transcript those credits earned for military service or for courses completed at other higher educational institutions. Professors and college administrators sometimes do not ensure that veterans receive credit for their military training and military experiences. Schools also fail sometimes to provide a student-veteran with adequate information about credit-transfer procedures during an institution's orientation session.

Abusive Academic Advising

The school does not provide veterans after entering college with appropriate tutoring in academic skills or in course material. A college's explanations of a student's curriculum sometimes do not address how veterans might design a plan of study. Advisors at a school sometimes do not know about military occupational specialties (MOS) and do not provide career advice that takes account of the student's MOS. The school does not take into account a veteran's military occupational specialty when advising veterans on what courses to take.

Abusive Teaching Practices

Some professors teach incorrect information or knowledge to student-veteran students. At this school some professors give veterans a brush off or ignore them in class or after class. Some professors make slanderous comments about military service in a class taken by student-veterans, where the comments can be shown to be irrelevant to course material. At this school some professors fail to give students academic help once the professors know these students are veterans.

Some professors and administrators proudly boast about anti-military activities that they engaged in during the Vietnam War or other war era. Additionally some younger professors also may express anti-military attitudes. Some professors and college administrators falsely claim to have rehabilitated themselves and to treat veterans of today fairly.

Abusive Course Practices of Professors

Some professors give a lower grade to student veterans than indicated by his or her class performance (that is, they give a student-veteran a lower grade than a non-veteran student who achieved the same academic performance as the student veteran). A student-veteran may not be allowed to finish an 'incomplete' that originated because the course was interrupted by deployment. Like some professors at a school, some administrators may make anti-military or anti-veteran comments to students knowing they are veterans.

An unsatisfactory grade is sometimes given to a student-veteran who is in the Guard or reserve because of absence for weekend or monthly military training. Current systems forawarding grades at some schools make it possible to award an unsatisfactory grade for a course that was not completed because the student-veteran was severely wounded or killed. Additionally, the grading system at some schools may make it possible to fail to overlook awarding a posthumous degree to a student-veteran who made the ultimate sacrifice in the student's senior year and to fail to present this degree to the student-veteran 's next of kin.

Abusive Practices of Administrators

Some schools do not provide veterans with access to their records. As a result, veterans can be asked to pay for incorrect billing for their education. The school may fail to return tuition and fees to a student-veteran for courses dropped because of deployment.

Some schools fail to provide veteran students part time employment in the same manner as provided to non-veterans. Many schools fail to provide veterans with access to a grievance program that is as easy as the access non-veterans have their grievance program. Sometimes an administration may fail to provide efficient administrative service to a student-veteran who returns from deployment.

Abusive Employment Placement

A school's career center is supposed to conduct an employment search for soon-to-be or new graduates. However, some career centers conduct an employment search for new graduates in a manner that does not consider military backgrounds of veterans. Additionally, most career center counselors are not familiar with resources to help veterans find jobs (such as employers who are veterans, and military-related web sites, such as VeteranEmployment.com, Military Connection, Military Exits, and Military Job Zone). In summary, the career center of most schools offers less help to veterans than to non-veterans on how to find a job.

Financially Abusive Practices of College Administrators

Administrators may not have access to data on service members and veterans to help higher education administrators anticipate the enrollment choices of returning veterans and military personnel. Some colleges suspend student-veterans for non-payment of tuition and fees when the non-payment is the result of bureaucratic problems in the federal agency, state agency or private organization that is supposed to make the payment.

Sometimes veterans have difficulty getting their GI Bill educational benefits paid to them. Often administrators do not have the data necessary to set forth the services needed to accommodate these student veterans under the new GI Bill. Most schools do not offer scholarships and/or grants to veterans. Many schools fail to provide a student-veteran with adequate information about how to apply for financial aid. Also most colleges do not provide assistance in finding financial support for veterans who have a family.

Medical Abuse of Veterans and Service members

Abusive Medical Practices by College Medical Staff.
Some schools do nothing to help students who have physiological and emotional disabilities that have been determined to be service connected by the VA. Most schools' health services will not treat a veteran on an emergency for a disability that may have arisen because of military service. The health services of most schools refuse to treat veterans unless they are enrolled in the health program for students. A school may fail to refer a student-veteran correctly to where proper medical care can be obtained such as at nearby Veterans clinics or hospitals.

Even if a veteran is enrolled in the school's health program, the staff is often unprepared to treat the wounds, diseases, or disorders of veterans. Professors, college administrators and college health center staff lack education in the health challenges of veterans in academic settings concerning the following challenges: Traumatic Brain Injury; Post Traumatic Stress Disorder (PTSD}; Emotional problems (Adjustment disorders, Depression, Suicide). Despite the lack of training, staff at some health centers will attempt to treat the veteran.

Conclusions About Abuse at a Particular School

In the absence of protected class status for veterans, a conclusion about abuse at a particular school is arbitrary and up to whomever is drawing the conclusions. Surveys have been conducted about how often certain kinds of abuse occur on campus. These surveys indicate that individual veterans usually do not encounter abusive practices very frequently. The abusive practices identified on surveys total about 60 different educational abuses and 9 administrative abuses on college campuses.

Surveys also have indicated that only a minority of schools are involved in administrative abuse. In a study of 723 schools, only about 31% of the schools reported some complaints from service members and veterans. The percentage of schools reporting particular kinds of complaints on another survey was: 25% concerning difficulties in obtaining transfer credits; 23% concerning how educational programs were not responsive to them; 19% concerning a campus climate that was unfriendly to those with a military background; 17% concerning difficulties in adjusting socially on campus; 8% concerning administrative difficulties that arose when they were deployed; 15% concerning difficulties in getting health care on campus. Another survey of more than 100 schools found that 30 percent of four-year public institutions, 35 percent of public community colleges, and 43 percent of private not-for-profit four-year colleges and universities reported that they did not provide services to veterans/service members.

Depending on one's background, these percentages are not high. However, it could be argued that these percentages should be close to zero. Certainly a protected class law would lead these percentages to be close to zero.

Veteran-Friendly Schools

Veterans want to study at the most veteran-friendly school that provides the education of the specialty that a veteran wants. These schools arrange to have their GI Bill paid to veterans without difficulty. Service members can assume that abuse is minimal at veteran friendly schools. However even some of these colleges have some professors and college administrators who abuse veterans.

A veteran-friendly school informs veterans about their educational programs. The non-veterans on campus are friendly toward veterans. The health services of veteran-friendly schools treat the emergency needs of veterans' service-connected medical problems. The career centers conduct employment searches for soon-to-be or new graduates in a manner that takes account of the graduate's military background, as well as the veteran's major or minor. Veterans are awarded academic credits for their military credits without having to fight the schools for these credits. These schools may also offer some scholarships and/or grants to veterans.

Veteran-Unfriendly Schools

These schools usually do not advertise that they want veterans. Professors, administrators, staff and non-veteran students do not go out of their way to help student veterans.

Some of these professors and administrators proudly boast about their anti-military beliefs and, if applicable, the protests that they engaged in during the Vietnam era.

These schools offer few if any of the rights, benefits and help that veterans have at veteran-friendly schools. Unfriendly schools typically offer no scholarships to veterans and their educational programs do not take account of veteran status. Advisors do not know about military occupational specialties and do not provide career advice that takes account of a student's military background. The health services of veteran-unfriendly schools refuse to treat emergency needs of veterans' medical problems unless they are enrolled in the health program for students. Career centers of these schools do not consider military backgrounds of veterans when conducting an employment search for soon-to-be or new graduates.

Link to the Vietnam War. Most senior members of academia recognize that they and/or their colleagues abused veterans during and after the Vietnam War. Some of these educators admit now that their previous abuse of Vietnam veterans was mistaken and that the object of their protest should have been the federal government. Because some of academia recognizes its abusive treatment of veterans after Vietnam was wrong, many of these educators claim to have made an effort to rehabilitate them and to now treat veterans fairly. Unfortunately, sometimes some educators still abuse veterans.

Conclusions About Whether the
Veterans at a School Need Protected Class Status

Undoubtedly professors and college administrators have the intellectual ability to mentally separate the acceptability of abuse of veterans from sound complaints about military practices, complaints that should be reported to leaders in our government.   Whether or not professors   and   college administrators will want to make this distinction in their thought processes remains to them. Whether or not educators will stop all abuse of veterans in higher education may depend   on legislators who might establish a protected class for veterans.

Chapter 5

Why Some Professors and College Administrators Abuse Veterans

A former director of the Service members Opportunity Colleges, Steve Kime, stated, "it is important to recognize that veterans' education is emerging from a poisonous environment that lasted more than a generation." This extremely negative past continues to undermine the college education of veterans today.

Professors and administrators should be taught to give respect to veterans for having given up freedoms and rights to serve in the public interest and defense. For example, veterans suffer excessive socially, economically, and educationally as a result of taking themselves out of the fabric of our comfortable national culture to serve in the military. Also veterans suffer significant social deprivation at some colleges for holding pro-military and patriotic beliefs. Professors and administrators would avoid accidental mistreatment of veterans if they would learn how to recognize veterans as accurately and as courteously as they recognize members of protected classes.

Anti-Veteran Beliefs of
Today's Abusive Educators

There are various reasons why some college educators abuse veterans. It is worthwhile to describe why some educators engage in such abuse in order to convince these college staff members to stop engaging in such abuse. If the causes of abusive behavior of educators are identified, then ways to discourage such abuse can be developed.

The professors and college administrators who abuse veterans apparently do so because they believe that such abuse is warranted in an effort to persuade government leaders to stop ongoing wartime activities. The beliefs that veterans and service members should be abused began during the Vietnam era and apparently have continued through the present wartime era. This is analogous to punishing a child for the misbehavior or faulty guidance of the parents. One does scream at, punish or belittle a child (or should not) for the mistakes of the parents. Likewise, military personnel and veterans are not the culprits of war; they are the tools of war, doing their tasks as the college staff members are doing theirs.

Professors and college administrators, in general, do not engage in abuse because these educators dislike their country. Most educators care as much about the longevity of our nation as any other group in society. Some of the educators who conduct abuse do so in an effort to seek peace. In this sense, an educator is like a soldier who above all other people prays "for peace, for he must suffer and bear the deeper wounds and scars of war" (General Douglas McArthur).

Some educators do not recognize that their abuse constitutes discrimination against veterans. These educators do not recognize that their abuse puts veterans at a disadvantage relative to non-veteran students. However, some of these educators were trained to disrespect anyone engaged in wartime activities. They hold contempt for members of the military and veterans that borders on hate. Groups of educators abuse veterans today because of beliefs held by each of these groups. These groups are listed below along with the reasons that the group chooses to abuse veterans.

Educators with Anti-Veteran Attitudes Established During the Vietnam War

1 - Senior Educators who Protested the Vietnam War. Some senior educators who abuse student veterans protested the Vietnam War when they were young. They continue to hold anti-military beliefs because they feel that their protest may dissuade our nation from engaging in all wars. Similarly, many of these senior educators had adopted anti-war beliefs because of the spirit of anti-military protest that was prevalent at that time. Because these senior educators formed anti-military attitudes when they were young; many of them still hold these attitudes. Many of these senior educators are retired or near retirement.

2 – Senior Educators who participated in the Vietnam Draft-Deferment Program. A number of anti-military senior educators today studied to become teachers through the draft deferment program of the late 1960's. It has been alleged that some of these individuals became college educators to avoid having to fight in Vietnam. More antimilitary educators are active today than would have been the case had the draft deferment program not existed.

Other wars in this century (such as World War I, World War II, the Korean War) did not lead protestors to become college educators because there were no draft deferment programs during those wars. Fewer educational categories permitted exclusion from military service or other avenues of serving during those wars. Some Vietnam protestors were not given a draft deferment because the draft deferment program was stopped before these students could sign up for the program. Later the draft was terminated.

3 – **Middle aged and Younger Educators Trained by Protestors of the Vietnam War.** Some middle age and younger educators also abuse veterans today because they adopted anti-military beliefs of senior educators who supervised these middle age and younger educators as they sought and obtained tenure. Like the senior educators, the middle age and younger educators also feel that their protest may dissuade our nation from engaging in a war that would be bad for our country or from even engaging in any military action.

Educators with Negative Attitudes about the Academic Abilities of Veterans

1 - Some college educators, professors and/or college administrators, abuse veterans because they believe that veterans are incapable of completing an higher education as provided in America. Veterans are assumed to be incapable of such an education because veterans originate from the lower classes that are believed to be dumb by these educators, i.e., the veterans and military personnel have fewer cognitive resources than these collegiate educators. The veterans and the military personnel are held to possess an "military mind."

2 - Some college educators abuse veterans because they believe that veterans are not capable of succeeding in higher education because the veterans and/or military personnel chose other than a college preparatory program in high school.

Educators with Negative Attitudes about War

1) - Some college educators abuse veterans because they believe that current war(s) are not justified. To

discourage any war efforts, veterans are abused in the hope that the abuse will render service members and veterans disinclined to fight the enemy. Furthermore, they believe that veterans who encounter abuse will be discouraged from re-enlisting.

2) - Some professors and/or college administrators abuse veterans because they believe that no war(s) is justified. These educators are pacifists.

3) - Some educators believe that liberalism entails being against war. The belief that liberals oppose war more than conservatives appears to have originated in the anti war movement during the Vietnam era. This liberal belief disposes some liberals to oppose any war, including the present ones.

Recent research demonstrates clearly that far more liberals than conservatives teach and administer in higher education. Professors with a liberal viewpoint tend to teach their courses from this liberal perspective. Thus, when an educator abuses veterans, that educator is more likely to be liberal than conservative. However, there is nothing in liberalism or conservatism that supports or warrants anti-war activity. For example, instead of being opposed to war, liberals were in favor of the revolutionary war and World War II. An example of this is Senator George McGovern who flew 35 missions as a B-24 pilot in the low-level precision daylight bombing campaign of Eastern Europe yet was advocating exit from Vietnam. This number of missions was significantly beyond the quota for rotation from the front and away from the highest risk of death of any type of service in World War II. One might say that McGovern hated war, but he hated other things more (our enemies in World War II).

Hard as it is to believe, some professors and college administrators may be truly unpatriotic. These educators want any military action of our country to fail. Some anti-patriotic educators existed in World War II and thereafter, so it seems possible that such educators exist today. These educators may not recognize that their beliefs constitute treason.

Anti-Veteran Abuse Ignored
by Non-abusive Educators

Abuse that is overlooked is not neutral. Overlooked abuse can serve to facilitate the abuse by educators who are active in the abuse. Some people think that being a bystander renders them a passive observer. However, ignoring abuse requires effort and affects how others view the abuse. Below are some examples of how overlooked abuse still results in more abuse.

Educators Who Abuse Veterans

1) - Some professors and administrators abuse veterans but do not talk about their negative behavior to prevent others from learning about this abuse.

2) - Some professors and administrators abuse veterans but do not talk about their negative behavior to avoid being criticized by those who abstain from engaging in abuse of veterans.

Educators Who Do Not Abuse Veterans

1) - Some professors and administrators do not abuse veterans, but they approve of the abuse.

2) - Some professors and administrators do not abuse veterans but, while they approve of this abuse, they do not want to make the effort that abuse requires.

3) - Some professors and administrators do not abuse veterans but they do not realize that their silence on abuse may be seen as approval of abusive behavior.

4) - Some professors and administrators do not abuse veterans but are aware of abuse of veterans by others. However, they do not talk about the abuse because they do not see it as their responsibility to help abused veterans.

The Consequences of Abuse

Abuse Interferes with the Education of Veterans and Service Members.

If abusers were aware that some colleagues disapproved of veteran abuse, some of these abusers might desist abusing. In some cases, verbal abuse may lead to unfair professorial practices such as giving veterans and service members' unsatisfactory grades for satisfactory academic performance. The administrative abuse may involve not giving veterans and service members educational services that they are required by law to receive. Abuse due to inadequate medical practices provided to veterans can be expected to interfere with the health of student-veterans.

Because of the Abuse Veterans Encounter, Too Few of Them Attend and Complete College

The difficulties veterans experience when attending and completing college are clearly evident in available statistics. Approximately 65%of the general population has had some college education and 29% of the general population has obtained a Bachelor's or higher degree. In contrast, approximately 41 % of veterans attend college and 15 % of veterans obtain a Bachelor's or higher degree. The current estimate of veterans attending college, 41.9% represents a recent increase in veterans who are receiving a college education.

Previous estimates of veterans obtaining some college were about 24% (approximately 40% of veterans used their educational benefits for some kind of education, from the end of World War II through the end of the Vietnam War). As noted above, the VA currently reports greater percentage of veterans attend college. Undoubtedly, even with increased interest in promoting a college-education for veterans, a substantially smaller proportion of veterans than the proportion of non-veterans attend college or graduate. The lower number of veterans attending college demands an explanation. The most obvious explanation of the low attendance is the abuse encountered by veterans.

The abuses of veterans by American higher education will be an embarrassment to our nation it if other nations who are our allies learn about this abuse. Moreover, our enemies would be pleased to learn that some of America's educators make obtaining a college degree much harder for veterans than it needs to be. Our enemies would be pleased to know that the abuse by some of our educators counteracts the substantial funds spent to try to educate our veterans. Our enemies also would be pleased to know that the morale of service members is decreased when they, and our veterans, learn about the abusive practices toward student-veterans who attend college. Furthermore, the enemies of the US would be pleased to know that decreases in the morale of our service members render them less safe in combat.

Chapter 6

Preventing the Abuse of Veterans
While in College

Veterans attend college because they seek:

1.   sophistication of skills,

2.   civilian careers that will provide them with a good living,

3.   to support themselves and their families, and

4.   to gain new insights about the world, themselves, and/or a body of knowledge to provide for others beyond themselves.

The review of media in Chapter 3 (and listed in the bibliography) found that many sources, written by a variety of authors and distributed by an array of publishers, have reported that some professors and/or administrators in some colleges abuse some veterans, making the attainment of their goals more difficult.

The review in Chapter 4 showed that veterans encounter a wide variety of abuses in college. The review in Chapter 5 showed that professors and administrators abuse veterans have a variety of reasons for engaging in such abuse. Some educators apparently abuse veterans because they believe that such abuse may persuade government leaders to terminate ongoing wartime activities. Other educators may do so because they believe that veterans are unprepared for college and that educators want to stop veterans from distracting educators who want to give their attention to other students.

Our military has successfully defended us for more than 220 years. However, no nation has survived indefinitely. To survive further, our nation needs to maintain a reliable and prepared military force. Service members and student-veterans should be treated as well as other students for protecting us or as potential heroes because they have stood ready to defend the U.S. if necessary. They certainly should not be punished for their military service.

This chapter proposes what might be done to eliminate educator abuse of veterans. First, the chapter considers how to eliminate abuse by convincing leaders in higher education to stop such abuse. Second, the chapter considers ways to change the beliefs of educators in a manner that the new beliefs would discourage educators from engaging in abuse. Thirds, the chapter addresses legal procedures that might penalize institutions for continuing to permit educator abuse of service-members and veterans.

Convince Educators that Their Ethics
Conflict with Abuse of Service members and Veterans

Abuse of those with an honorable military background is immoral. It is morally wrong to abuse those who have defended, or agreed to defend, the nation at large. The mission of professors, college administrators, and staff is to provide all students with a good education. No legitimate code of ethics directs educators to isolate and abuse those who have served in our military.

Abuse That Hinders Academic Performance of Veterans is Immoral. It is ironic that American society invests significant funds into the education of service members and veterans, when much of these funds are wasted while veterans seek a college degree are hampered by those charged with assisting all students genuinely.

The stress experienced by veterans on campus by harassment from instructors and staff interferes with the veterans' academic performance because abuse causes veterans to lose study time, perform less well in courses, and obtain lower grades. The abuse that veterans encounter in higher education clearly undermines their ability to succeed academically.

Abuse Interferes with the Responsibility of Educators to give Service Members and Veterans the Best Higher Education Possible. Schools, their professors and administrators, have a responsibility to educate members of our military so that our nation will succeed and prosper. Students with a military career ahead need to be given the best education possible so that they can learn to repair and operate the latest military equipment, perform strategic use of the equipment, and interact effectively with allies. Veterans need a college or technical education to ensure a swift and complete transition to civilian careers. The best education is needed as well to ensure that service members and veterans maintain a good morale. There is no need in higher education for educators and academic institutions to be unfriendly to service members and veterans.

Prohibiting Veteran Abuse in Higher Education

Educators need to Adopt Philosophic Beliefs that are Inconsistent with the Abuse of Service members and veterans. As discussed in Chapter 5, most professors and college administrators usually have a liberal background. Liberalism is believed by some educators to entail that they be against war in general. However, educators should be taught that liberalism does not entail automatically and without exception that he or she should be anti-war. The motivation of most anti-war educators is to obtain peace but most historians recognize that some wars are necessary, such as World War II.

Establishing Veterans as a Protected Class could stop the discrimination and abuse of veterans. Veterans who have survived any conflict do not deserve to be verbally, administratively, or medically abused. They do not deserve to be subjected to any practice that makes it hard to succeed academically. If protected class status of veterans were established, it would be against the law for professors, college administrators, staff and even non-veteran students to abuse veterans.

Individual educators guilty of discrimination or abuse of a student veteran should be punished for their abusive behavior suspended or terminated. Schools convicted of abuse should also be fined and lose funds awarded to a school for research, special education programs or veterans programs. In some cases, an abusive school could lose accreditation.

Alternatively, more incentives should be established for individual educators and schools that demonstrate a track record for supporting, mentoring, welcoming service members and veterans. Currently there are several incentive programs (federal, state, and corporate) to support and guide schools in higher education to treat veterans fairly. As long as schools get funds that serve as incentives, the schools will try to treat veterans fairly. However, unless professors and administrators at a school benefit from an incentive scheme, or the veterans become a protected class, the collegiate setting might remain as harsh as it sometimes is currently for those with military status of any kind.

If protected class status were not established for veterans, certain negative practices could persist at the national, school or individual level. For example, it should be illegal for a school to ask veterans (or anyone) to sign a contract that obligates the veterans financially for the total cost of an education. Currently some proprietary schools impose such an obligation on veterans. Another example of a practice that should be illegal is when a school fails to refer a student-veteran correctly to proper medical care (including counseling) at nearby Veterans clinics or hospitals. A third practice is to recruit a student for a specific program that is attractive to the student. The school then enrolls the student, making the student obligated financially for the fees. Afterward, the student is informed that this program, which was offered, is no longer available and that the student has to enroll again in another program. If veterans held protected class status, schools would stop engaging in such abusive practices.

Abuse that Originates in Hate or Prejudice. Sometimes veterans are abused because they are the objects of hate on campus (discussed in Chapter 5). Some college educators, professors and/or college administrators, abuse veterans also because they believe that veterans are not sufficiently intelligent or prepared to succeed in higher education. Similarly, some college educators, professors and/or college administrators, abuse veterans because they believe that veterans are incapable of succeeding in higher education because most veterans did not take a college preparatory program in high school.

A Flaw in the Logic that Educators Use to Justify their Abuse of Veterans

Because veterans and service members represent war or potential war, many educators feel they are justified in expressing critical views of war to those who have served in the military. Unfortunately, there is a clear mistake in logic evident here. Veterans and service members do not choose when, where, or how to engage in war. They just carry out the orders of the President and the Congress. Therefore, anti-military actions toward veterans and military personnel are misguided and groundless.

When sexual harassment was made illegal, educators were taught why their abuse of women or men was groundless. Similarly, educators should be taught why their harassment of veterans is abusive. Educators should be taught that (1) veterans do not formulate the orders to aggress against an enemy, (2) that the Congress and executive branch formulate such orders, and (3) that anyone who wants to change the orders that the military follows should persuade Congress and the executive branch to changes such orders. Educators should not assume that their role is to harass the military or former members of the military, i.e. veterans.

Today's veterans need legal protection now. Even if the number of abused veterans may not be large, none of our past and present members of the military deserve abuse. Regulations should be established that prohibit educators from abusing veterans. Educators should know that a uniform does not give a service member protection against abuse in college for the same reason that physical and cultural characteristics of currently protected class members do not protect them from abuse; the law provides this protection and consequences for those who ignore that law.

Recent Regulations Prohibit Colleges and Universities from Requiring Veterans to Reapply for Admission after being Absent for a semester due to Military orders.

These regulations were passed in 2009. A partial version of them are presented below. These regulations were developed after many veterans had been unfairly denied readmission after they returned from deployment and attempted to re-enroll in their college. The regulations specify the conditions that must hold for both the veteran and the higher educational institution when a veteran is allowed to continue as a student at the school the veteran attended prior to being absent for military service. An Abbreviation of the regulation is as follows:

"VETERANS' READMISSION"
Final Regulations
October 29, 2009

Citation: 34 CFR § 668.18.
Federal Register/ Vol. 74, No. 208/ Thursday, October 29, 2009 (Approved by the Office of Management and Budget under control number 1845 NEW1) (Authority: 20 U.S.C. 1088 et seq.) **Final Regulations (pp. 55934-36)**. Section 668.18 Readmission requirements for service members is added to subpart B of part 668 to read as follows:

"(a) *General.* (1) An institution may not deny readmission to a person who is a member of, applies to be a member of, performs, has performed, applies to perform, or has an obligation to perform, service in the uniformed services on the basis of that membership, application for membership, performance of service, application for service, or obligation to perform service.

(2)(i) An institution must promptly readmit to the institution a person with the same academic status as the student had when the student last attended the institution or was last admitted to the institution, but did not begin attendance because of that membership, application for membership, performance of service, application for service, or obligation to perform service.

(ii) ``Promptly readmit'' means that the institution must readmit the student into the next class or classes in the student's program beginning after the student provides notice of his or her intent to reenroll, unless the student requests a later date of readmission or unusual circumstances require the institution to admit the student at a later date.

(iii) To readmit a person with the ``same academic status" means that the institution admits the student--

(A) To the same program to which he or she was last admitted by the institution or, if that exact program is no longer offered, the program that is most similar to that program, unless the student requests or agrees to admission to a different program;

(B) At the same enrollment status that the student last held at the institution, unless the student requests or agrees to admission at a different enrollment status;

(C) With the same number of credit hours or clock hours completed previously by the student, unless the student is readmitted to a different program to which the completed credit hours or clock hours are not transferable;

(D) With the same academic standing (e.g., with the same satisfactory academic progress status) the student previously had; and

(E)(1) If the student is readmitted to the same program, for the first academic year in which the student returns, assessing—

(i) The tuition and fee charges that the student was or would have been assessed for the academic year during which the student left the institution; or

(ii) Up to the amount of tuition and fee charges that other students in the program are assessed for that academic year, if veteran's education benefits, as defined in section 480 (c) of the HEA, or other service member education benefits, will pay the amount in excess of the tuition and fee charges assessed for the academic year in which the student left the institution, or

(2) If the student is admitted to a different program, and for subsequent academic years for a student admitted

to the same program, assessing no more than the institutional charges that other students in the program are assessed for that academic year.

(iv)(A) If the institution determines that the student is not prepared to resume the program with the same academic status at the point where the student left off, or will not be able to complete the program, the institution must make reasonable efforts at no extra cost to the student to help the student become prepared or to enable the student to complete the program including,   but not limited to,   providing refresher courses and allowing the student to retake a pretest at no extra cost.

(B) The institution is not required to readmit the student on his or her return if--

(1) After reasonable efforts by the institution, the institution determines that the student is not prepared to resume the program at the point where he or she left off;

(2) After reasonable efforts by the institution, the institution determines that the student is unable to complete the program; or

(3) The institution determines that there are no reasonable efforts the institution can take to prepare the student to resume the program at the point where he or she left off or to enable the student to complete the program;

(C)(1) ``Reasonable efforts'' means actions that do not place an undue hardship on the institution.

(2) ``Undue hardship'' means an action requiring significant difficulty or expense when considered in light of the overall financial resources of the institution and the impact otherwise of such action on the operation of the institution.

(D) The institution carries the burden to prove by a preponderance of the evidence that the student is not prepared to resume the program with the same academic status at the point where the student left off, or that the student will not be able to complete the program.

(3) This section applies to an institution that has continued in operation since the student ceased attending or was last admitted to the institution but did not begin attendance, notwithstanding any changes of ownership of the institution since the student ceased attendance."

The remainder of these regulations provide a variety of contingencies that limit the required readmission. These limitations are concerned with the duration of deployment, the timeliness of a reapplication and practical constraints that preclude a school from providing the readmission.   The regulations presented above have been passed with additional details. A reader who is interested in these limitations on readmission can find them discussed in a full copy of the regulation.

New Regulations Needed

Veterans need the support of more regulations of higher education.   Certain potential regulations were recently proposed to the Veterans Affairs Committee of Indiana.   These regulations were proposed to protect the higher education of students who are service members or student veterans (SV) from unfair biased practices of professors and college administrators. These potential regulations have yet to be proposed to the Indiana legislature. These regulations would make illegal the abuse of four categories if approved by the legislature.

I. Abusive Practices of Professors During a Semester

- To give a student-veteran a lower grade than indicated by his or her class performance (that is, to give a student-veteran a lower grade than a non-veteran student who achieved the same academic performance as the student-veteran)

- To award an unsatisfactory grade to a student-veteran because of absence for military training
- To make negative comments about military service in a class taken by student-veterans unless the negative comments can be shown to be relevant to course material
- To teach information or knowledge known to be incorrect to one or more student-veterans
- To provide a student-veteran with incorrect advice about courses to be taken for a major, minor, electives, or general education requirements

II. Abusive Practices of Professors Concerning Deployment of Student-Veterans
- To deny a student-veteran the opportunity to complete a course interrupted by deployment
- To deny a student-veteran the opportunity to finish an 'incomplete' that originated because the course was interrupted by deployment
- To deny a student-veteran the opportunity to achieve an adequate grade for finishing an 'incomplete' that originated because the course interrupted by deployment
- To award an unsatisfactory grade for a course that was not completed because the student-veteran made the ultimate sacrifice
- To fail to award a satisfactory grade for a course that was not completed because the student-veteran suffered diseases, wounds, or disorders in his or her military service
- To fail to present to a student-veteran's next of kin a satisfactory grade for a course taken by a student who made the ultimate sacrifice
- To fail to award a posthumous degree to a student-veteran who made the ultimate sacrifice in the student's senior year
- To fail to present to a student-veteran's next of kin a posthumous degree awarded to the student who made the ultimate sacrifice in the student's senior year

III. Abusive Practices of College Administrators During a Semester

- To not award an institution's credits to a student-veteran's transcript for those credits earned by the student-veteran for military service or for courses completed at other higher educational institutions
- To refuse to give a student-veteran proper medical care equivalent to that which would be given to all students for an acute condition
- To refer a student-veteran incorrectly to where proper medical care (including counseling) presumably may be obtained (including nearby clinics or hospitals of the VA)
- To provide a student-veteran with inadequate information during a higher educational institution's orientation session (to provide less essential information to a student-veteran than is provided to non-veteran students)
- To provide a student-veteran with inadequate information about how to apply for financial aid (that is, to spend less time trying to find financial aid for an student-veteran than the time spent for finding aid for a non-veteran student)
- To suspend student-veterans for non-payment of tuition and fees when the non-payment is the result of bureaucratic problems in the federal, state agency or private organization that is supposed to make the payment
- To fail to provide as much assistance to student-veteran graduates in seeking employment as provided to non-veteran students

IV. Abusive Practices of College Administrators Concerning Deployment

- To require a student-veteran to drop a course taken at the time of deployment
- To fail to return tuition and fees to a student-veteran for courses dropped because of deployment
- To fail to provide efficient administrative service to a student-veteran who returns from deployment

Appropriate Complaints
Of the Military and/or Of Military Action

Sometimes professors and administrators have good reasons to complain about the government's use of the military and/or about military practices.   Under our system of government, citizens can freely make complaints about the behaviors of members of our military without fear of reprisal. Still, if those with complaints about actions of the military abuse veterans, then such abuse should be illegal. Those with complaints should direct those complaints to members of our federal government, congress and agencies.

Ways for Educators to Lodge Valid Complaints About Military and/or Diplomatic policy

- Write to your senator, congressperson, president, Joint Chiefs, DOD, VA, and Department of Education.
- Donate funds to the political party whose policy of which you approve.
- Join the party whose veterans-education policy you approve of.
- If there is an organization that protests the policy, join it
- If there is not an organization that protests the policy, form one.

Ways for Educators to Find Help from Veterans-service organizations to Stop Educational Abuse of Veterans

Thirteen new veterans organizations have been formed since 9/11 or have formed a policy to help veterans who have encountered abuse in college.

Academic Veterans Association (AVA)
Vietnam Veterans Institute (VVI)
Student Veterans of America (SVA)

College Educators for Veterans Higher
    Education (CEVHE)
Veterans Communities at Institutions of Higher
    Learning
Operation Diploma
Supportive Education for Returning Veterans
Veteran and Military Programs and Services
Operation Vets
Indiana Higher Educators
Indiana ESGR
Iraq and Afghanistan Veterans of America
Veterans for Education
Veterans for America
Veterans Education Project
Wounded Warriors: STEM

Educators can Find Help from Higher Education organizations in Stopping Educational Abuse of Veterans. Higher education is assisted with a variety of matters by government and private organizations. These organizations include, among others, the American Council on Education, the American Association of University Professors, and the Association of Colleges and University Administrators. These organizations possess expertise that could be marshaled to eliminate many of the college problems of veterans.

Justice in American Higher Education

Elimination of discrimination and abuse of student veterans is in the best interests of our nation. Veterans who survive military service, with or without disabilities, possess wisdom and courage. It is in the best interest of our nation to educate as many veterans as possible so that they are available to contribute and, if need be, lead in the special way that only veterans can. In summary, a college or university can help create a better environment for educating veterans throughout America by prohibiting any kind of discrimination of abuse of service members and veterans.

Veterans have experience that has prepared them to lead our country in various ways: in our community, in the professions and in state and national politics. However, as long as professors and college educators abuse veterans, fewer young people will enlist. Among those that do join the military, fewer veterans and service members feel that they have a future or at least not a very promising one after they leave the military. If one is a veteran, how can one feel positive about the future when those in the education profession want to shut the door on him or her? If educators cannot respect those who defend them, whom can educators respect?

Some educators wonder why the suicide rate is so high among service members and veterans. Educators need to put themselves in the shoes of veterans of Iraq and Afghanistan to empathize with those veterans who have risked death, who have wondered if they would live through the night, who have thought that they would never see their families again, who became angry seeing that what they were risking was unimportant to those at home who were untouched by the wars and threats of harm or death.   How would an educator feel after having risked life and limb only to have the door to higher education closed by those who were protected? How would anyone feel after having lost friends and seen some friends maimed for life only to know have the door to the higher education of their friends closed by those who were protected?   It is no wonder that some service members and veterans give up on their future.

Retribution

If educators were made aware of the terrible consequences to veterans caused by their abuse – however big or small, some educators   might   cease abusing them. Suppose that educators were subjected to the same abuse to which veterans have been subjected.   For example, suppose that a group of non-educators decided that educators do not deserve respect and even deserve disrespect.   Such a reversal of maltreatment is not too far fetched.   It is a fact that some members of our society disrespect educators.   For example, some members of the trades – plumbers, electricians; and some professions – lawyers, journalists; and some members of the military do not respect college educators.   This disrespect is increasing because many of today's college graduates cannot find a job and because those in the trades are seeing their occupations exported to China, Mexico and other off-shore locations.

How would veteran-abusing educators feel if they were abused by a group of anti-educators in the same manner as anti-veteran educators abuse veterans?   Suppose that anti-educators make an effort to interfere with efforts of individuals as they try to become educators. Here are some examples of possible abuse of educators.

When College Educators seek the Education required to obtain a job as a Professor or College Administrators. College educators acquire their specialty by studying in an appropriate program in graduate school. These days the majority of college educators have a doctorate (a PhD). Some few have a Master's degree.   Suppose that aspiring educators were provided with incorrect advice by anti-educators about what courses are needed to get an appropriate graduate degree. For example, the anti-educator group might disseminate pamphlets with incorrect information about courses to be taken by future educators. Disseminating incorrect information to future educators is comparable to today's educators providing veterans with incorrect information about the requirements for a major, minor, or gen-ed courses. If treated in a similar way, the anti-veteran educator may recognize that it is wrong to provide incorrect information to veterans.

Alteration of Academic Credit Records. When professors and college administrators apply for educational jobs, their resume could be altered by anti-educators so as to present incorrect records of courses taken by the educators. [Veterans often take more courses than necessary because they find it difficult to get administrators to give them the right transfer credits].

Employment Application of Educators. Suppose that potential employers, guided by anti-educators, provide educators with false job requirements, salary and employment benefits when they apply for a job. [Veterans are often given little information about the jobs to which they apply on or after graduation].

New Employee Training Given to Educators. An employer may fail to ease the transition of new educators to their academic jobs by not explaining the college's programs, services and policies. [Veterans are often given little or no orientation to the schools they attend].

Verbal Abuse of New Educators. The established employees at a school might be unfriendly to new educators and say insulting things about the background of these new educators. [Veterans encounter non-veteran students who say negative things to new student-veterans].

Abusive Training Practices. Some trainers may ignore recently hired educators after a training session. Some trainers may proudly boast about their past anti-educator activities. [Many veterans have encountered similar treatment from some of today's educators].

Abusive Evaluation Practices of Trainers. Anti-educator trainers may give an educator a lower evaluation of his or her training performance than actually occurred. For example, an unsatisfactory training score might be given to an educator who had missed training because he or she had to attend a meeting at the direction of the employer. Also an unsatisfactory training score might be awarded when an employee did not finish training because he or she became ill for the latter part of training. Anti-educator employers may fail to award benefits to the kin of a worker who passed away while working on the job. [Veterans encounter similar maltreatment from anti-veteran educators].

Abusive Practices for Performance Assessment. New educators need feedback about their job performance to improve their work habits. However, if an employer's explanations of an employee's specialty are incorrect, the employee is not able to learn how to handle his or her new job. [Veterans have difficulty learning a course because they are sometimes given incorrect grades for their course performance].

Abuse of Educators by Administrators. Educators might not be provided salary for their work by anti-educator supervisors. [Sometimes veterans are not provided funds that they are supposed to be paid for work done on campus, work-study hours, and other tasks done and allegedly compensated].

Abusive Employment Placement Practices. Human resource staff with anti-educator bias may fail to conduct an employment search for educators who are terminated for reasons not pertaining to the performance of these educators. [Veterans receive less help from career centers than non-veteran students].

Abusive Financial Practices. Educators may have difficulty getting their salary paid to them by anti-educator administrators. Educators may also have difficulty getting a raise that should accompany a promotion by anti-educators. [Veterans receive less federal help from the GI Bill because some bureaucrats in some schools do not ensure that veterans are provided these funds].

Abusive Health Practices of Anti-Educators. Suppose that the staff of an employer's health center consists of anti-educators who do not know how to treat the known wounds, diseases, or disorders of employees who are educators. [Veterans often encounter health centers that try to avoid treating the health problems of veterans].

Conclusions About Anti-Educator Abuse

Many more examples may be developed about of how educators might be abused by anti-educators. Today's educators may want to consider whether discrimination and abuse of veterans is the right thing to do. Now may be the time for anti-veteran educators to stop abusing veterans.

**Ending Higher Education's
Abuse of Veterans**

The simplest way to put an end to the abuse of veterans by higher education is to make veterans a "protected class." If it were illegal to abuse veterans in any manner, a professor and college administrator would stop abusing any veteran. Recently President Obama set forth in April of 2012, an Executive Order that essentially makes all manner of abuse of veterans illegal. However, executive orders are enforceable only as long as the president who established the order is in office, and longer if subsequent presidents enforce the order.

Below is a copy of President Obama's Executive Order concerning veteran abuse in higher education. This Executive Order has been disseminated poorly; so many educators may not know that abuse of veteran is now illegal.   Letting our colleagues in teaching and college administration know about this Executive Order is a first step toward establishing a protected class for veterans in the short term.

For Immediate Release   April 27, 2012

EXECUTIVE ORDER

ESTABLISHING PRINCIPLES OF EXCELLENCE FOR EDUCATIONAL INSTITUTIONS SERVING SERVICE MEMBERS, VETERANS, SPOUSES, AND OTHER FAMILY MEMBERS

By the authority vested in me as President by the Constitution and the laws of the United States of America, and in order to ensure that Federal military and veterans educational benefits programs are providing service members, veterans, spouses, and other family members with the information, support, and protections they deserve, it is hereby ordered as follows:
Section 1. Policy. The original GI Bill, approved just weeks after D-Day, educated nearly 8 million Americans and helped transform this Nation. We owe the same obligations to this generation of service men and women as were afforded that previous one. This is the promise of the Post-9/11 Veterans Educational Assistance Act of 2008 (title V, Public Law 110-252) (Post-9/11 GI Bill) and the continued provision of educational benefits in the Department of Defense's Tuition Assistance Program (10 U.S.C. 2007): to provide our service members, veterans, spouses, and other family members the opportunity to pursue a high-quality education and gain the skills and training they need to fill the jobs of tomorrow.

Since the Post-9/11 GI Bill became law, there have been reports of aggressive and deceptive targeting of service members, veterans, and their families by some educational institutions. For example, some institutions have recruited veterans with serious brain injuries and emotional vulnerabilities without providing academic support and counseling; encouraged service members and veterans to take out costly institutional loans rather than encouraging them to apply for costly institutional loans rather than encouraging them to apply for Federal student loans first; engaged in misleading recruiting practices on military installations; and failed to disclose meaningful information that allows potential students to determine whether the institution has a good record of graduating service members, veterans, and their families and positioning them for success in the workforce.

To ensure our service members, veterans, spouses, and other family members have the information they need to make informed decisions concerning their well-earned Federal military and veterans educational benefits, I am directing my Administration to develop Principles of Excellence to strengthen oversight, enforcement, and accountability within these benefits programs.

Sec. 2. Principles of Excellence for Educational Institutions Serving Service Members, Veterans, Spouses, and Other Family Members. The Departments of Defense, Veterans Affairs, and Education shall establish Principles of Excellence (Principles) to apply to educational institutions receiving funding from Federal military and veterans educational benefits programs, including benefits programs provided by the Post-9/11 GI Bill and the Tuition Assistance Program. The Principles should ensure that these educational institutions provide meaningful information to service members, veterans, spouses, and other family members about the financial cost and quality of educational institutions to assist those prospective students in making choices about how to use their Federal educational benefits; prevent abusive and deceptive recruiting practices that target the recipients of Federal military and veterans educational benefits; and ensure that educational institutions provide high-quality academic and student support services to active-duty service members, reservists, members of the National Guard, veterans, and military families.

To the extent permitted by law, the Principles, implemented pursuant to section 3 of this order, should require educational institutions receiving funding pursuant to Federal military and veterans educational benefits to:

(a) prior to enrollment, provide prospective students who are eligible to receive Federal military and veterans educational benefits with a personalized and standardized form, as developed in a manner set forth by the Secretary of Education, working with the Secretaries of Defense and Veterans Affairs, to help those prospective students understand the total cost of the educational program, including tuition and fees; the amount of that cost that will be covered by Federal educational benefits; the type and amount of financial aid they may qualify for; their estimated student loan debt upon graduation; information about student outcomes; and other information to facilitate comparison of aid packages offered by different educational institutions;

(b) inform students who are eligible to receive Federal military and veterans educational benefits of the availability of Federal financial aid and have in place policies to alert those students of their potential eligibility for that aid before packaging or arranging private student loans or alternative financing programs;

(c) end fraudulent and unduly aggressive recruiting techniques on and off military installations, as well as misrepresentation, payment of incentive compensation, and failure to meet State authorization requirements, consistent with the regulations issued by the Department of Education (34 C.F.R. 668.71-668.75, 668.14, and 600.9);

(d) obtain the approval of the institution's accrediting agency for new course or program offerings before enrolling students in such courses or programs,

provided that such approval is appropriate under the substantive change requirements of the accrediting agency;

(e) allow service members and reservists to be readmitted to a program if they are temporarily unable to attend class or have to suspend their studies due to service requirements, and take additional steps to accommodate short absences due to service obligations, provided that satisfactory academic progress is being made by the service members and reservists prior to suspending their studies;

(f) agree to an institutional refund policy that is aligned with the refund of unearned student aid rules applicable to Federal student aid provided through the Department of Education under Title IV of the Higher Education Act of 1965, as required under section 484B of that Act when students withdraw prior to course completion;

(g) provide educational plans for all individuals using Federal military and veterans educational benefits that detail how they will fulfill all the requirements necessary to graduate and the expected timeline of completion; and

(h) designate a point of contact for academic and financial advising (including access to disability counseling) to assist service member and veteran students and their families with the successful completion of their studies and with their job searches.

Sec. 3. Implementation of the Principles of Excellence.

(a) The Departments of Defense and Veterans Affairs shall reflect the Principles described in section 2 of this order in new agreements with educational institutions, to the extent practicable and permitted by law, concerning participation in the Yellow Ribbon Program for veterans under the Post-9/11 GI Bill or the Tuition Assistance Program for active duty service members. The Department of Veterans Affairs shall also notify all institutions participating in the Post-9/11 GI Bill program that they are strongly encouraged to comply with the Principles and shall post on the Department's website those that do.

(b) The Secretaries of Defense, Veterans Affairs, and Education, in consultation with the Director of the Bureau of Consumer Financial Protection (CFPB) and the Attorney General, shall take immediate action to implement this order, and, within 90 days from the date of this order, report to the President their progress on implementation, including promptly revising regulations, Department of Defense Instructions, guidance documents, Memoranda of Understanding, and other policies governing programs authorized or funded by the Post-9/11 GI Bill and the Tuition Assistance Program to implement the Principles, to the extent permitted by law.

(c) The Secretaries of Defense, Veterans Affairs, and Education shall develop a comprehensive strategy for developing service member and veteran student outcome measures that are comparable, to the maximum extent practicable, across Federal military and veterans educational benefit programs, including, but not limited to, the Post-9/11 GI Bill and the Tuition Assistance Program. To the extent practicable, the student outcome measures should rely on existing administrative data to minimize the reporting burden on institutions participating in these benefit programs. The student outcome measures should permit comparisons across Federal educational programs and across institutions and types of institutions. The Secretary of Education, in consultation with the Secretaries of Defense and Veterans Affairs, shall also collect from educational institutions, as part of the Integrated Postsecondary Education Data System and other data collection systems, information on the amount of funding received pursuant to the Post-9/11 GI Bill and the Tuition Assistance Program. The Secretary of Education shall make this information publicly available on the College Navigator Website.

(d) The Secretary of Veterans Affairs, in consultation with the Secretaries of Defense and Education, shall provide to prospective military and veteran students, prior to using their benefits, streamlined tools to compare educational institutions using key measures of affordability and value through the Department of Veterans Affairs' eBenefits portal. The eBenefits portal shall be updated to facilitate access to school performance information, consumer protection information, and key Federal financial aid documents. The Secretaries of Defense and Veterans Affairs shall also ensure that service members and veterans have access to that information through educational counseling offered by those Departments.

Sec. 4. Strengthening Enforcement and Compliance Mechanisms. Service members, veterans, spouses, and other family members should have access to a strong enforcement system through which to file complaints when institutions fail to follow the Principles. Within 90 days of the date of this order, the Secretaries of Defense and Veterans Affairs, in consultation with the Secretary of Education and the Director of the CFPB, as well as with the Attorney General, as appropriate, shall submit to the President a plan to strengthen enforcement and compliance mechanisms. The plan shall include proposals to:

(a) create a centralized complaint system for students receiving Federal military and veterans educational benefits to register complaints that can be tracked and responded to by the Departments of Defense, Veterans Affairs, Justice, and Education, the CFPB, and other relevant agencies;

(b) institute uniform procedures for receiving and processing complaints across the State Approving Agencies (SAAs) that work with the Department of Veterans Affairs to review participating institutions, provide a coordinated mechanism across SAAs to alert the Department of Veterans Affairs to any complaints that have been registered at the State level, and create procedures for sharing information about complaints with the appropriate State officials, accrediting agency representatives, and the Secretary of Education;

(c) institute uniform procedures for referring potential matters for civil or criminal enforcement to the Department of Justice and other relevant agencies;

(d) establish procedures for targeted risk-based program reviews of institutions to ensure compliance with the Principles;

(e) establish new uniform rules and strengthen existing procedures for access to military installations by educational institutions. These new rules should ensure, at a minimum, that only those institutions that enter into a memorandum of agreement pursuant to section 3(a) of this order are permitted entry onto a Federal military installation for the purposes of recruitment. The Department of Defense shall include specific steps for instructing installation commanders on commercial solicitation rules and the requirement of the Principles outlined in section 2(c) of this order; and

(f) take all appropriate steps to ensure that websites and programs are not deceptively and fraudulently marketing educational services and benefits to program beneficiaries, including initiating a process to protect the term "GI Bill" and other military or veterans-related terms as trademarks, as appropriate.

Sec. 5. <u>General Provisions</u>. (a) This order shall be implemented consistent with applicable law and subject to the availability of appropriations.

(b) Nothing in this order shall be construed to impair or otherwise affect:

(i) the authority granted by law to an executive department, agency, or the head thereof; or

(ii) the functions of the Director of the Office of Management and Budget relating to budgetary, administrative, or legislative proposals.

(c) This order is not intended to, and does not, create

any right or benefit, substantive or procedural, enforceable at law or in equity by any party against the United States, its departments, agencies, or entities, its officers, employees, or agents, or any other person.

BARAK OBAMA

Passage of a protected class law for veterans would provide them with legal protection that will be in force beyond the executive order established by President Obama or a subsequent president.

Epilogue

Surveys indicate that the number of educators who abuse veterans is small. The vast majority of college professors and administrators are dedicated to imparting the latest knowledge to their students. Regardless of what they think about war or current military action, most would never abuse any student to vent these feelings. America's educators are ethical and want to see that veterans are treated well and in the same manner as non-veteran students. When they become aware that a student is being abused in some manner, they will take the necessary steps to prevent this mistreatment.

Nevertheless, whenever it occurs, abuse of veterans and service members should not be tolerated. Educators who become bystanders of such abuse should report it. Professors, administrators, deans, provosts, presidents and chancellors have the capability to persuade abusive educators to stop mistreating veterans, to inform abusive educators to express any of their negative feelings about war to elected officials, and to ask educational organizations (such as accrediting bodies) to punish such abuse. The likelihood that veterans and service members are abused should be no greater than the likelihood that non-veterans are abused.

As discussed in the previous chapter, grants have been established to discourage veteran abuse. Likewise, federal and state laws have been created that are aimed at better treatment of veterans. However grants and existing laws have not been enough to prevent abuse of veterans. The best way to ensure equality in the abuse of veterans and non-veterans is to pass a law that establishes veterans and service members as a protected class. We hope that educators throughout America will do what they can to establish such a law.

Bibliography

Below are the references for books, magazine articles, journals, power point files, and PDF files that are relevant for each chapter. These references are presented as they would be in a reference section to an article or book about a source that focuses on certain information. Some of the references are cited under more than one chapter. To save space in the overall book, references are typed in a smaller font (8 pt) than the rest of the text (12pt).

Most references are formatted below according to the style of the American Psychological Association. The goal has been to put as much information as possible in a reference to enable readers to find the reference on the Web. Readers are forewarned that there might be some typos or wording problems in some references because the contents of this bibliography have been assembled from a variety of sources over several years. Readers can access these references by searching the web or the contents of a college or university library.

References for Chapter 1 concerning Protected Class Status

Equal Employment Opportunity (EEO) (2011) Definition of EEO Terminology for Protected Class. Discrimination may result when rules and policies are applied differently to members of protected classes. Disciplining Hispanic and Afro-American employees.

Macias, W. (2010). Non-Tech Higher Education Rights. US Dept. of Education (Office of Postsecondary Education).

Rechenberg, D. N. (2009). Rechenberg, D. N. (2009). Title VII Checklist. FRANKS & RECHENBERG, P.C., 1301 Pyott, Road Suite 200, Lake in the Hills, Illinois 60156

Welfley Cordesman, J. (2010) Federal Government Is Contemplating a New Protected Class. Millisor & Nobil Co., LPA

Wikipedia, the free encyclopedia (2011). Protected class, a term used in United States anti-discrimination law. The term describes characteristics or factors that cannot be targeted for ... · http://en.wikipedia.org/wiki/Protected_class - Cached

Zimmerman, J. (2007). The Liberal (and Moderating) Professoriate. Inside Higher Ed, October.

References for Chapter 2 concerning Protected Class for Veterans

Armstrong, K., Best, S. & Domenici, P. (2005). Courage After Fire: Coping Strategies for Returning Soldiers and Their Families. Berkeley, CA: Ulysses Press.

Columbian (2007) The Vietnam 'Gorilla.' Vancouver, WA. Retrieved on September 28th from http://panther.indstate.edu:2048/login?url=http://search.ebscohost.com/login.asp?direct=true&db=nfh&AN=2W62W64081430012&site=ehost-live.

Equal Employment Opportunity (EEO) (2011) Definition of EEO Terminology for Protected Class. Discrimination may result when rules and policies are applied differently to members of protected classes. Disciplining Hispanic and Afro-American employees.

Gamlem, C. (2000). Workforce Challenges for the Twenty-First Century. Written for the Society of Human Resource Management.   In a book   "Visions of the Future: HR Strategies for the New Millennium."

Gordon, J. E. (2010). Protected Class Status and Veterans. In J. Hopkins, D. Herrmann, R. Wilson, B. Allen & L. Malley (Eds). Improving the College Education of Veterans. Charleston, S. C.: CreateSpace.

Judish, J. E. & Heaven, J. N. (2008). Department of labor completes updates to veteran's affirmative action rules. Employment and Labor. Pillsbury, Winthrop, Shaw, & Pittman.

Krueger, A.B. & Angrist, J. D. (2007). The All-Volunteer Military: Issues and Performance. Congressional Budget Office, July.

Macias, W. (2010). Non-Tech Higher Education Rights. US Dept. of Education (Office of Postsecondary Education).

Malamud, O. & Wozniak, A. (2010).   The Impact of College Education on Geographic Mobility: Identifying Education Using Multiple Components of Vietnam Draft Risk. College mobility and the Vietnam draft.pdf.

Michigan Tech University Definition of Protected Classes (2010). Protected class groups are a group of people protected from ... Veterans covered under 41 CFR 60-250 of the Vietnam Era 'Veteran's Readjustment Assistance Act. see http://www.admin.mtu.edu/aao/protectedclass.htm - Cached.

Miller, L. A., Herrmann, D., & Rouse, R. A.. (2010). "Top Gun" Institutions of Higher Education: A Military-Focused Educational Profile Separating the Best from the Rest. University of Phoenix Research Institute.

North Carolina University (2007). Seminars on how veterans are a protected class. Retrieved on December 11, 2008 from http://www.ncsu.edu/equal_op/education/oeo_programs.html.

Proskauer Rose LLP. (2004). Veterans Gain Protected Status in Massachusetts. Client Alert, October. http://www.mass.gov/legis/laws/seslaw04/sl040355. From http://www.mass.gov/legis/laws/seslaw04/sl040355.

Rechenberg, D. N. (2009). Title VII Checklist. FRANKS & RECHENBERG, P.C., 1301 Pyott, Road Suite 200, Lake in the Hills, Illinois 60156

U.S. Equal Employment Opportunity Commission (2000). Policy Guidance on scope of Veterans' Preference Under Title VII of the Civil Rights Act of 1964, as amended, 42 U.S.C. ∂ 2000e. ORIGINATOR. Title VII/EPA Division, Office of Legal Counsel.

Vietnam Era Veterans Readjustment Assistance Act (1974). (VEVRAA): Veterans covered under 41 CFR 60-250 of 1974 (VEVRAA):

Welfley Cordesman, J. (2010) Federal Government Is Contemplating a New Protected Class. Millisor & Nobil Co., LPA

Wikipedia, the free encyclopedia (2011a). Protected class, a term used in United States anti-discrimination law. The term describes characteristics or factors that cannot be targeted for ... http://en.wikipedia.org/wiki/Protected_class - Cached

Wickipedia, the free encyclopedia (2011b). Conscription.doc. Jan 21,pdf

Wickipedia, the free encyclopedia (2011c). Liberalism in the United States. pdf.

Wikipedia, the free encyclopedia (2010). Containment in the Vietnam war. pdf

Yates, J. E. & Herrmann, D. (2010) A White Paper on Protected Class Status for Veterans. American Legion Annual Meeting, February.

Zimmerman, J. (2007). The Liberal (and Moderating) Professoriate. Inside Higher Ed, October.

References for Chapter 3 include following four kinds of publications that address verbal and administrative abuse of student veterans. Ch. 3 [1] Books about abuse of veterans by higher education. Ch. 3 [2] Historic books/ pamphlets about veterans abuse. Ch. 3 [3] Articles about veteran abuse in higher education. Ch. 3 [4] Surveys about veterans abuse in higher education.

Ch 3. (1) Books that address abuse against Veterans by Educators in Colleges and Universities

Ackerman, R. & DiRamio, D. (Eds.) (2009). In Creating a Veteran-Friendly Campus: Strategies for Transition and Success New Directions for Student Services, No. 126, Wiley Periodicals.

Anderson, R. C. (2004). Home front: The government's war on soldiers. Atlanta: Clarity Press.
http:www1.va.gov/vso/inde.cfm?template=viewreport&Org.ID=338-13k-Cached

Committee on Academic Standards (2010). New Standards Provide a Framework for Establishing College Veterans Services Programs. Franklin, D.

Cook, B. J. , & Kim. Y. (2009).   From Soldier to Student: Easing the Transition of Service Members on Campus. Lumina Foundation.

DiRamio, D. & Jarvis, K. (2011). Veterans in Higher Education. Wiley Periodicals. Hoboken, N.J.

Herrmann, D. J. Hopkins, C., Wilson, R. B. & Allen, B. (2011). Progress in Educating veterans in the 21st Century. North Charleston, South Carolina: Create Space.

Herrmann, D. J. Hopkins, C., Wilson, R. B. & Allen, B. (2009). Educating veterans in the 21st Century. North Charleston, South Carolina: BookSurge.

Herrmann, D., Schooler, C., Caplan, L. J., Lipman, P. D., Grafman, J.,Schoenbach, C., Schwab, K., & Johnson, M. L. (2001). The latent structure of memory: A confirmatory factor-analytic study of memory distinctions (results of the Vietnam Head Injury project). Multivariate Behavioral Research, 36, 29-5

Hopkins, C., Herrmann, D. J., Wilson, R. B., Allen, B., & Malley, L. (Eds.) (2010). Improving College Education of Veterans. North Charleston, South Carolina: Create Space.

Mettler, S. (2005). Soldiers to citizens: The GI Bill and the Making of the Greatest Generation. Cambridge: Oxford Univ. Press.

Powers, J. T. (2008a). Campus Kit for Colleges and Universities. Student Veterans of America. Retrieved from www.studentveterans.org.

Powers, J. T. (2008b). Campus Kit for Student Veterans. Student Veterans of America. Retrieved from www.studentveterans.org

Roth-Douquet, K. & Schaeffer, F. (2006). AWOL: The Unexcused Absence of America's Upper Classes from Military Service — and How It Hurts Our Country, New York: Collins.

Schram, M. (2008) Veterans under siege: How America Deceives and dishonors those who fight our battles. New York: St. Martins. See http://www.veteransforamerica.org/home/vfa/

Schupp. J. (2011) The Higher Education of Veterans. The writings of John Schupp. Cleveland, Ohio.

Servicemembers Opportunity Colleges. (2004). What is SOC? Retrieved onFebruary 5, 2005, from http://www.soc.aascu.org/socgen/WhatIs.html.

Sternberg, M., MacDermid Wadsworth, S., Vaughan, J., & Carlson, R. (2009). The higher education landscape for student service members and veterans in Indiana. West Lafayette: Military Family Research Institute at Purdue.

Stiglitz, J. E. & Bilmes, L. J. (2008) The Three Trillion Dollar War: The True Cost of the Iraq Conflict. New York: Norton, W. W. & Company.

Tick, E. (2005). War and the Soul Healing our Nation's Veterans from Post traumatic Stress Disorder. Wheaton, Ill: Theosophical Publishing House.

Vincennes University (2008) Military Education Program Handbook: Arkansas Edition. Vincennes, Indiana 47591 from www.vinu.edu/military

Washton, N. S. (1945) A veteran goes to college: Opinions of a soldier who has been a college teacher. *Journal of Higher Education*, 16, No. 4 (Apr., 1945), pp. 195-196,226

Wenger, D., Rufflo, M., & Bertalan, F. J. (2006). ACME project, internet-based systems that advocate credit for military experience and analyze options for veterans in career transition. Proceedings of the IEEE International Conference on Advanced Learning Techniques, IEEE The Computer Society.

Wilson, R. B. & Herrmann, D. (2012) Veterans College Handbook. North Charleston, South Carolina: Create Space.

Chap 3 (2) - Books/pamphlets of an historic nature on veterans by higher education.

Avery, C. E. (1946). Veterans' education in the universities. Journal of Higher Education, 17, 360.

Bedford, J. H. (1946) The veteran and his future job. Los Angeles: Society for Occupational Research.

Bolte, C . G. (1945) The new veteran. New York: Reynal & Hitchcock.

Cartright, M. A. (1944). Marching home: Educational and social adjustment after the war. New York: Teachers College, Columbia University.

Clark, D. A. (1998). "The two Joes meet—Joe college, Joe veteran" History of Education Quarterly, 38, 166-189.

Commission on Post-War Training and the Adjustment (1942). A statement of principles relating to the educational problems of returning soldiers, sailors, and displaced war industry workers. New York: Teachers College, Columbia University.

Dillingham, W. P. (1952) Federal aid to veterans. Gainsville: University of Florida Press.

Educational Policies Commission (1944). A program for the education of returning veterans. Washington, D.C.: National Education Association of the United States and the American Association of School Administrators.

Fine, B. (1947). Veterans raise college standards. Educational Outlook, 22, November.

Frederiksen, N. (1951). Adjustment to College: A study of 10,000 Veteran and Nonveteran Students in Sixteen American Colleges. Educational Testing Service: Princeton, NJ.

Gaines, F. P. (2004). 1945 opening the doors of opportunity: liberal education and the veterans. Liberal Education, Fall.

Lipsett, L. & Smith, L. F. (1949). Veterans carry through on operation "education." Journal of Educational Research, *42*, 395-397.

Love, L. L. & Hutchison, C. A. (1946). Academic Progress of Veterans. Educational Research Bulletin, 25, 223-226.

Rogers, C. R. & Wallen, J. L. (1946) Counseling returned servicemen. New York: McGraw Hill.

Rollins, P. C. (1993) Behind the Westmoreland Trial of 1984. Journal of the Vietnam Veterans Institute, 2, No. 1.

Ross, D. B. (1969). Preparing for Ulysses: politics and veterans during World War II. NewYork.

Severo, R. & Milford, L. (1990). The Wages of War: When America's soldiers came home – from Valley Forge to Vietnam. New York: Touchstone.

Todd, W. E. (1949). Rehabilitation and education for veterans of World War II. Stanford University Bulletin, Dissertation Abstracts, ser 8(35).

Verkamp, V. J. (1992). The moral treatment of returning warriors in early medieval and modern times. Scranton, Pennsylvania: University of Scranton Press.

Webb, R. W. & Atkinson, B. H. (1946). The Veteran is in College. The Journal of Higher Education. XVII, *5*, 238-242, 282.

Wector, D. (1944). When Johnny comes marching home. Boston: Houghton Mifflin.

Weller, W. W. (1944). The veteran comes back. New York: Dryden Press.

Chap 3 [3] - magazine articles, journal articles, chapters, web publications, PDF files, and videos about higher educational abuse of veterans.

Ackerman, R., DiRamio, D., & Garza Mitchell, R. L. (2009) Transitions: Combat veterans as college students. In Ackerman, R. & DiRamio, D. (Eds.) Creating a Veteran-Friendly Campus: Strategies for Transition and Success. New Directions for Student Services, No. 126, Jossey Bass:

Ackerman, R. & DiRamio, D. (Eds.) (2009). In Creating a Veteran-Friendly Campus: Strategies for Transition and Success New Directions for Student Services, No. 126, Wiley Periodicals.

Adams, J. A. (2000). The G.I. bill and the changing place of higher education after World War II. Presented at the annual meeting of the Association for the Study of Higher Education. Sacramento, CA., November.

Administrator of Polish News (2008). Rep. Rahm Emanuel and representatives from Chicago-area universities today announced policies that will make it easier for veterans of the wars in Iraq and Afghanistan to attend college in Illinois and succeed, Polish news. Tuesday, 19 August. Retrieved on March 26, 2009 from http://www.polishnews.com/index.php option=com_content&view=article&catid=81:news-from-chicago-wiadomoci-z-chicago&id=359:emanuel-chicago-area-universities-unveil-first-in-the-nation-plan-to-utilize-new-gi-bill-send-veterans-to-college-&Itemid=198

Aleethia Foundation (2007) The Aleethia Foundation supports recently injured troops in their rehabilitation upon returning home. Retrieved on November 22, 2008 from http://www.humanevents.com/article.php?id=23076 - 50k; see also http://www.aleethia.org/

Allen, B. S., (2003). Comments welcome veterans home, Readjustment Counseling Service, Vet Center Voice, 24, p. 29. US Department of Veterans Affairs, Washington, DC.

Allen, B.S., (Ed.), (1987).   Now and Then Magazine,. 4, #3. Center for Appalachian Studies and Services, East Tennessee State University, Johnson City, Tennessee.

Allen, B. S. Jr., Herrmann, D., & Giles, S. L. (1995). Vietnam as a class war: Myth or reality. Sociological Spectrum, 14, 299-311

American Association of Collegiate Registrars and Admissions Officers (AACRAO) (2008) Retrieved from http://www.aacrao.org

American Council on Education (ACE) (2011). Schools that want to be vet friendly can find out how at this web site: http://www.vetfriendlytoolkit.org/

American Council on Education (ACE) (2009), American Association of Small of Student Affairs Administrators in Higher Education Administrators: From Soldier to Student. American Council on Published by the American Council on Education for Military Programs: Washington D.C.

American Council on Education. (ACE) (2008a). Serving those who serve: Higher education and America's veterans. Retrieved March 5, 2009, from http://www.acenet.edu/Content/NavigationMenu/ProgramsServices/MilitaryPrograms/serving/Veterans_Issue_Brief_1108.pdf

American Council on Education (ACE) (2008b). Student Veterans Speak Out About Their College Experience: Senator Hagel Frames Discussion on Veterans and Higher Education. Conference on "Serving Those Who Serve: Higher Education and America's Veterans" Georgetown University. June 5.

American Council on Education (ACE) (2008c) Severely Injured Military Veterans ACE supported a Fulfilling Their Dreams project in which veterans with severe injuries are assisted in their return to civilian life. Retrieved on March 20, 2009 from http://www.acenet.edu/Content/NavigationMenu/Programs_Services/MilitaryPrograms/veterans/index.htm-69k-Cached-Similar pages

American Council on Education (ACE) (2008d). A Transfer Guide: Understanding Your Military Transcript and ACE Credit Recommendations. Military Programs: Washington D.C.

American Council on Education (ACE) (2007), Military installation voluntary education review orientation and guidelines.   Retrieved in January 2003. http://www.acenet.edu/AM/Template.cfm?Section=Search§ion=PDF6&template=/CM/ContentDisplay.cfm&ContentFileID=300.

American Council on Education (ACE)(2004). Military programs. Retrieved February 21, 2003 from http://www.acenet.edu/calec/military.

American Council on Education (ACE) and Wal-Mart Team-up (2008). ACE and Wal-Mart Team-up to Offer Veteran Grants – Education. Retrieved on March 20, 2009 from http://www.military.com/money-for-school/ace-and-wal-mart-team-up--to-offer-veteran-grants - 18k

Anderson, D. L. (2002). The Columbia guide to the Vietnam War. New York: Columbia University Press.

Anderson, R. C. (2004). Home front: The government's war on soldiers. Atlanta: Clarity Press.

Angrist, J. D. (1993). The effect of veterans benefits on education and earnings. Industrial & Labor Relations Review, 46, 637-653.   Anonymous, VFW. (2001). House votes G.I. Bill Raise, Ups Ante on Senate. Retrieved in 2007 from http://acenet.edu/calec/military

Anonymous, VFW. (2001). House votes G.I. Bill Raise, Ups Ante on Senate. Retrieved in 2007 from http://acenet.edu/calec/military

Anonymous, VFW (2007a). Applauds Disability Benefits Commission Report. Executive summary and full report. Retrieved on September 10 http://www.vetscommission.org/reports.asp

Anonymous. VFW. (2007b). Educational attainment and war vets. Veterans of Foreign Wars Magazine, 94, 8-9.

Appy, C. (1992). Working Class War, University of North Carolina Press.

Armstrong, K., Best, S. & Domenici, P. (2005). Courage After Fire: Coping Strategies for Returning Soldiers and Their Families. Berkeley, CA: Ulysses Press.

Asch, B. J., Kilburn, M. R., & Klerman, J. A. (1999). Attracting college-bound youth into the military: toward the development of new recruiting policy options. Rand Mongraph (Number: MR-984-OSD): RAND Distribution Services. http:// www.rand.org/about/

Ashby, C. M. (2002). Veterans' education benefits: comparison of federal assistance awarded to veteran and non-veteran students. Report to the Ranking Minority Member on Committee on Veterans Affairs. U.S. Senate by the Director of Education, Workforce and Income Security, U.S. General Accounting Office,

Association of Veterans Education (2006). Association of Veterans Education Certifying Official. A Non-Chartered Organization. National Headquarters Address, 9813 104th Avenue Ottumwa, IA 52501. Retrieved from http:www1.va.gov/vso/inde.cfm?template=viewreport&Org_ID=338 - 13k - Cached

Bascetta, C. A. (2002). Military and veterans' benefits: observations on the transition assistance program. Testimony before the Subcommittee on Benefits Committee on Veterans' Affairs, House of Representatives. Washington, DC: General Accounting Office (GAO-02-914T).

Bauman, M. (2009) The mobilization and return of undergraduate students serving in the National Guard and Reserves. In Ackerman, R. & DiRamio, D. (Eds.), Creating a Veteran- Friendly Campus: Strategies for Transition and Success New Directions for Student Services, No. 126, Jossey Bass: San Francisco.

Bauerlein, M. (2004). Liberal groupthink is anti-intellectual. Chronicle of Higher Education, November 12, 2004.

Baechtold, M. & De Sawal, D. M. (2009). Meeting the needs of women veterans. In Ackerman, R. & DiRamio, D. (Eds.), Creating a Veteran-Friendly Campus: Strategies for Transition and Success. New Directions for Student Services, No. 126, Jossey Bass: San Francisco.

Beacon, J. E. (2008). Proposal for one-time veteran's tuition waive. Terre Haute: Indiana State University.

Berry, G. L. (1977). Counseling needs of disadvantaged veterans. Journal of College Student Personnel, 18, 406-412.

Bhagwati, A. (2011), "A serious breach of ethics committed by the faculty and administration of the Columbia University School of Social Work against an Iraq war veteran, Sergeant First Class (SFC), Ret. Eli Painted Crow." See taken from McCaffrey's Facebook page. See also: anu@servicewomen.org "brad@lunamediagroup.com", "John D. Mikelson" <john-mikelson@uiowa.edu>

Black, T., Westwood, N. J., Sorsdal, M. N., & Michael. M. N. (2007). From the Front Line to the Front of the Class: Counseling Students Who Are Military Veterans. In J. A. Lippincott and R. A. Lippincott, Ruth A. (Eds.) Special populations in college counseling: A handbook for mental health professionals. (pp. 3-20). Alexandria, VA: American Counseling Association.

Boscarino, J. A., (2006) Eternal-cause mortality after psychological trauma: The effects of stress exposure and predisposition. Comprehensive Psychiatry, 47, 503-514.

Bound, J. & Turner, S. (2002). Going to War and Going to College: Did World War II and the GI Bill Increase Educational Attainment for Returning Veterans? Journal of Labor Economics. Chicago: Oct 2002. 20, Issue. 4; p. 784 (32 pages).

Brown, P. (2006, January 12). "Since we need both, DoD, academia must reconcile." The Orlando Sentinel. Retrieved on 20 Jan. 2006 from http://www.orlandosentinel.com.

Brown, W. (2011) Veterans For Education. Brian Teter, Disabled vet kicked out of college. Iraqi war veteran claims discrimination. http://video.foxnews.com/v/1181448445001/disabled-vet-kicked-out-of-college/?playlist_id=86856

Brown, R. (1998). Prejudice. Malden, Mass.: Blackwell Publishers.

Bureau of Labor Statistics (2006). College enrollment and work activity of 2006 high school graduates. USDL 07-0604 Washington DC: United Sates Department of Labor.

Butchjax (2005) To the anti-military recruiters. Retrieved on September 14, 2007 from   http://butchjax.wordpress.com/about/

Buyer, S. (2004). "Wall street and main street agree: Veterans give business the winning edge!" House Committee on Veterans' Affairs., March 24. Retrieved on Jan 12, 2006 from
http://veterans.house.gov/hearings/schedules108/mar04/3-24-04/witness/html.

Campbell, P. (2009) Problems of Veterans who are students in college. Executive Summary of Educating Veterans. Iraq and Afghanistan Veterans of America.

Campus Antiwar Network (2003). "independent, democratic, grassroots network of students opposing the occupation of Iraq and military recruiters in our schools."

Campus Antiwar Network (2004). March 2004, at City College of New York, four people were arrested at a counter-recruitment protest.

Card, D. & Lemieux, T. (2001). Going to college to avoid the draft: The unintended legacy of the Vietnam War. The American Economic Review, Vol. 91, No. 2, Papers and Proceedings of the Hundred Thirteenth Annual Meeting of the American Economic Association. (May, 2001), pp. 97-102.

Carney, C. P., Sampson, T. R., & Voelker, M. (2003). Women in the gulf war: combat experiences, exposures, and subsequent health care use. *Military Medicine, 168,* 654-661.

Caudell, R. (2005). Need a lift? To Educational Opportunities, Careers, Loans, Scholarships, & Employment. (54th edition). Indianapolis, IN.: American Legion National Headquarters. http://emblem.legion.org

Chicago Tribune (2009) Clout-Less: How University of Illinois Changed Admissions Procedures to Keep Military Veterans Out. May 9.

Clark, C. A (2004) State demographics and veteran disability. A Master's thesis in the field of government. Cambridge: Harvard University.

Clark, D. A. (1998). "The two Joes meet—Joe college, Joe veteran" History of Education Quarterly, 38, 166-189.

Cohen, J., Segal, D. R., & Temme, L. V. (1992). The impact of education on Vietnam-Era veterans. Social Sciences Quarterly, 73, 397.

Colloquy Live (2005). GI Recruiting Blues, Chronicle of Higher Education. May12th.

Committee on Academic Standards (2010). New Standards Provide a Framework for Establishing College Veterans Services Programs.

Columbian (2007) The Vietnam 'Gorilla.' Vancouver, WA. Retrieved on September 28th from http://panther.indstate.edu:2048/login?url=http://
search.ebscohost.com/login.asp?
direct=true&db=nfh&AN=2W62W64081430012&site=ehost-live

Congressional Research Service (2008). Report for Congress: American War and Military Operations Casualties: Lists and Statistics.

Cook, B. J. & Kim, Y. (2008) From Soldier to Student: Easing the Transition of Service Members on Campus. Lumina Foundation.

Cooper, A. (2007). Young veterans struggle to find jobs. Anderson Cooper Blog 360, CNN, April 4.

Council for Opportunity in Education (2008) ACE Launches New Veterans Initiative with help from WalMart. Retrieved from http://www.coenet.us/ecm/AM/
Template.cfm?Section=November_2008&Template=/CM/
HTMLDisplay.cfm&ContentID... - 39k

Crawley, J. W. (2006). Young vets can't find jobs. Potomac News. September 14, Retrieved on June 13, 2007 from http://www.potomacnews.com/servlet/Satellite?
pagename=WPN%2FMGArticle%2FWPN_Basic
Article=MGArticle&cid=1149188216054&path=

Defense activity for non-traditional education support agency. (2004). Voluntary education fact sheet fy03. Retrieved on June 9, 2005 from http://
www.dantes.doded.mil/dantes_web/library/docs/voledfacts/FY03.pdf.

Democracy Now (2005). Campus Resistance: Students Stage Counter-Recruitment Protests Across the Country. War & Peace Report on Democracy Now radio and TV show. Hosted by Amy Goodman and Juan Gonzalez http://www.democracynow.org/article.pl?sid=05/03/18/145022

Department of Veterans Affairs (2007). The post 9/11 Veterans Education Assistance Act of 2008. VA Pamphlet 22-09-1.

Department of Veterans Affairs (2006). Homeless veterans. Retrieved on September 12, 2007 from http://www1.va.gov/homeless/page.cfm?pg=1

Department of Veteran Affairs. (2004). National survey of veterans. Washington, D. C.: National Center for Information Analysis and StatisticsDO-IT (Disabilities, Opportunities, Internetworking, and Technology) (2009)

Department of Veteran Affairs (1994). *National Survey of Veterans.* Washington, D. C.: National Center for Information Analysis and Statistics.

DiRamio, D., Ackerman, R., & Mitchell R. L. (2008). From combat to campus: Voices of student-veterans. NASPA Journal, 45(1), 73-94.

DiRamio, D. & Spires, M. (2009) partnering to assist disabled veterans in transition. In Ackerman, R. & DiRamio, D. (Eds.), Creating a Veteran-Friendly Campus: Strategies for Transition and Success. New Directions for Student Services, No. 126, Jossey Bass: San Francisco. Published online in Wiley InterScience

Dobbs, J. M., Hopper, C. H., & Jurkovic, G. J. (1990). Testosterone and personality among college students and military veterans. Personality and Individual Differences, 11,1263-1269.

Donnelly, F. (2006). Today's GI bill: pay for it. Staten Island Advance. September 03. Retrieved on September 14 2007 from http://www.silive.com/news/advance/inde.ssf?/base/news/1157289309263610.ml&coll=1

Drew, D. E., & Creager, J. A. (1972). The Vietnam-era veteran enters college. Washington, D.C.: American Counsel on Education.
Drury, T. (2005). Really supporting our troops. Buffalo Business First. October 3. Retrieved Jan 14, 2006 from http://buffalo.bizjournals.com/buffalo/stories/2005/1003/focus1.htm l.

Dyhouse. T. (2004). GI bill needs 21st century upgrade. Veterans of Foreign Wars Magazine, 92, 4, 1.

Emmons, M. (2006). Traumatic brain injury: The 'Signature wound' of wars in Iraq and Afghanistan. Oakland Tribune. Retrieved Nov. 12, 2008. http://nl.newsbank.com/nlsearch/we/Archives=113840p]. Dec. 26, 2006.

Enzie, R. F., Sawyer, R. N., & Montgomery, F. A. (1973). Manifest anxiety of Vietnam returnees and undergraduates..Psychological Reports, 33, 446.

Eric. (2007). Homeless veterans are everywhere, but who's counting? Classical Values. September 8. Retrieved from September 14, 2007 from http://www.classicalvalues.com/archives/2007/09/post_449.html

Erickson, E. (2009) Congress votes to protect pedophiles, but not veterans (voted down that veterans could be the targets of hate crimes). Redstate.

Farrell, E. F. (2005). Military recruiters promise 'money for college', but recent veterans find that tuition benefits fall short. Chronicle of Higher Education. May 13.

Field, K. (2009). More Veterans May Attend 4-Year Colleges Full Time, Study Finds, August 27. Washington.

Fields, S. (2006). Who say college boys are smart? Townhall. November 6. Retrieved on December 15, 2006 http://www.townhall.com/columnists/SuzanneFields/2006/11/06/who_say_college_boys_are_smart

Figley, C. R. (1978). Symptoms of delayed combat stress among a college sample of Vietnam veterans. Military Medicine, 143,107-110.

Fogg-Davis, H. J. (2007). Understanding Affirmative Action: Politics, Discrimination, and the Search for Justice – by J. Edward Kellough. Governance; Vol. 20, p545-547.

Ford, D., Northrup, P., & Wiley, L. (2009) Connections, partnerships, opportunities, and programs to enhance success for military students. In Ackerman, R. & DiRamio, D. (Eds.), Creating a Veteran-Friendly Campus: Strategies for Transition and Success. New Directions for Student Services, No. 126, Jossey Bass: San Francisco.

Franklin, D. (2010) Committee on Academic Standards (CAS) Standards for Veterans and Military (3).pdf

Friedman, M.J. (2009). Post-traumatic stress disorder and suicidal behavior: A narrative review. Clinical Psychology Review, 29:6, 471-482. 11.

Gaines, F. P. (2004). 1945 opening the doors of opportunity: liberal education and the veterans. Liberal Education, Fall.

Gaul, B. (2006). Rigid, Command-and-Control Leadership? I don't Think So. Destiny Group. Retrieved on 10 Jan. from   https://destinygrp.com/destiny/template/ show_article.jsp?article_id=113.

Geraerts, E., Kozaric-Kovacic, D., Merckelbach, H., Peraica, T., Jelicic, M., & Candel, I. (2007) Traumatic memories of war veterans. Consciousness and Cognition: An International Journal, vol. 16, . 170-177.

Geiser Consent Decree (2001). Eecutive Order 11246, as amended to the Rehabilitation Act of 1973 and the Vietnam Era Veteran Readjustment Assistance Act. Retrieved from http://en.wikipedia.org/wiki/Eecutive_Order_11246http://en.wikipedia.org/wiki/ 1973_Rehabilitation_Act - 29k - http://www.dol.gov/compliance/laws/comp-vevraa.htm - 40k -

Gelber, S. (2005). A 'Hard-Boiled Order': the reeducation of disabled WWI veterans in New York City. Journal of Social History, Fall.

George, P. (2005). Group protests Army presence at career fair. The Daily Texan, University of Texas at Austin.   October 20th.

Gibbens, D. (2009). The Best Practices in Educating Veterans and Servicemembers. In Hopkins, C., Herrmanan, D. Wilson, Allen, B. & Malley, L. Improving College Education for Veterans. Charleston: Create Space.

Gillman, J. (2002) Students feign death in anti-war protest. Student newspaper at the University of Rhode Island. Issue date: 11/26/02 Section: News.

Gilroy, M. (2007). G.i. tuition benefits: What's right, what's wrong. The Hispanic Outlook in Higher Education, 17, 15-17.

Gimbel, C. & Booth, A. (1994). Does military combat experience adversely affect marital relations? Journal of Marriage & Family, 56, 691-703.

GI Rights Hotline (2007). Information to members of the military about discharges, grievance and complaint procedures, and other civil rights. Retrieved from http://www.objector.org/girights/contact.html

GoArmy.Com (2007). Retrieved in September, 2007 from www.goarmy.com/ rotc/enlisted_soldiers.jsp - 63k - Cached - Similar pages - Note this

Golden, D. (2006). Foreign Students Find U.S. Colleges To Be More Forthcoming With Aid. Wall Street Journal.: 3 Jan 2006. http:/ opendoors.iienetwork.org/?p=2947

Gordon, J. E. (2012a). Higher Education's Mistreatment of Veterans. Written with the Steering Committee for the Protected Class for Veterans. Unpublished manuscript. Available from Admiral Gordon or Douglas.Herrmann@gmail.com.

Gordon, J. E. (2012b). Descriptions of the Contents of Sources about higher education abuse of veterans prepared for Admiral Gordon by the Members of the Steering Committee for a Protected Class for Veterans (members of the Committee include M. Dakduk, T. Daywalt, D. Gibbens, J. Glasstetter, D. Herrmann, J. Mikelson, L. Miller, D. Raybeck, J., Schupp, W. Smith, M. Tomsey, R. Trewyn, R. B. Wilson, J. Yates), Unpublished manuscript available from Admiral John E. Gordon or Douglas.Herrmann@gmail.com.

Gordon, J. E. (2012c). How to Access Sources regarding Higher Education's Mistreatment of Veterans prepared for Admiral Gordon by the Members of the Steering Committee for a Protected Class for Veterans (members of the Committee include M. Dakduk, T. Daywalt, D. Gibbens, J. Glasstetter, D. Herrmann, J. Mikelson, L. Miller, D. Raybeck, J. Schupp, W.. Smith, M. Tomsey, R. Trewyn, R. B. Wilson, J. Yates), Unpublished manuscript available from Admiral John E. Gordon or Douglas.Herrmann@gmail.com.

Government Officials (2008). Educating Veterans on Entitled Benefits, Protecting Veterans' Rights, and Initiating Needed Reform (Inside the Minds). The Changing Landscape of Veterans Affairs, Aspatore Books Staff.

Greenberg, M. (2004). How the GI Bill changed higher education. The Chronicle of Higher Education. Washington: Jun 18, 2004. .50, B.9

Griffith, K. (2006). Young veterans face hurdles at home—Federal and local officials alarmed at unemployment rate in troops returning from Iraq. VA Watchdog. Retrieved on September 14 2007 from http://www.vawatchdog.org/old%20newsflashes %20AUG%2006/newsflash08-06-2006-9.htm

Hall, R. (2007). Protestors wrong on Vietnam, Then and on Iraq now. *CNS*. Retreved April 5, 2008

Hall, W. C. & Schweizer, P. (2005). Campus radicals vs. our vets. National Review Online. Retrieved Aug 29, 2005, from http://www.nationalreview.com/comment/hall_schweizer200508290810.asp

Harmeyer, E. (2007). Dartmouth President founds college service for wounded veterans. VFW Magazine, September, 18-19. Retrieved from http: www.vfw.org

Harris, J, T., III (2005). Higher education, college rankings and access for lower-income students. Black Issues in Higher Education. 21, 106.

Hartle, T. E. (2010), Improvements to the Post 9/11 GI Bill. American Council on Education before the Committee on Veterans Affairs, July 21st.

Heller, J. (2006). From Combat to College War Veterans on Campus. VFW Magazine, Retrieved from http: www.vfw.org

Hemingway, M. Z. (2007). Vets winning job suits. Federal Times, 43, p1-5.

Henderson, J. L. (1977). Persistence and nonpersistence of disadvantaged Vietnam-era veterans in college. Dissertation Abstracts International, 37, 4133-4134.

Herrmann, D. (2009). Indiana's Best Practices for the Higher Education of Servicemembers and Veterans. Veterans Higher Education Group. Terre Haute, Indiana.

Herrmann, D. J. (2007a) Investigations into the Treatment of Servicemembers by Indiana Higher Educational Institutions. Terre Haute, IN: Veterans Higher Educational Group.

Herrmann, D. (2007b). A Survey of Indiana Colleges and Universities about Concerns of Members of the Guard and Reserves About Problems in College. Terre Haute, IN: Veterans Higher Education Group, May.

Herrmann, D. (2007c). What it is like to be a veteran in college today. Presented to the Veterans Advisory Committee on Education. Washington, D.C. May.

Herrmann, D. & Yates, J. E. (2010) Protected Class Status for Veterans. American Legion annual meeting.

Herrmann, D. J., Raybeck, D., & Wilson, R. (2008). College Is for Veterans, Too. The Chronicle of Higher Education, November 21.

Herrmann, D., Schooler, C., Caplan, L. J., Lipman, P. D., Grafman, J.,Schoenbach, C., Schwab, K., & Johnson, M. L. (2001). The latent structure of memory: A confirmatory factor-analytic study of memory distinctions (results of the Vietnam Head Injury project). Multivariate Behavioral Research, 36, 29-51.

Higgs (2006). Wars and Numbers; Geocites; Retrieved in 2006 from www.geocities.com/Athens/Acropolis/2321/memorialday2003/number).

Higher Education Reconciliation Act (2005). Public Law 109-171; Title VIII of the Deficit Reduction Act, was approved by conference committee and subsequently approved by the Senate on December 21, 2005, the House on February 2, 2006 and signed by the President on February 8, 2006.

Hillen, J. (1999). Must U.S. Military Culture Reform? Orbis-Philadelphia, 43 (1), 43-58.

History News Network. (2003). How many American troops have died in war. Retrieved on September 14 2007 from http://hnn.us/articles/1381.html

Holder, K. A. (2007) The Educational Attainment of Veterans: 2007. US Census Bureau.

Horne, A. D. (1981). The wounded generation: America after Vietnam. Englewood Cliffs: Prentice Hall.

Hopkins, C. D. & Antes, R. L. (1990) Classroom Measurement and Evaluation (3rd ed.) Itasca, IL: F. E. Peacock.

House Committee On Veterans' Affairs (2001). H.R. 1291, 21st century. Montgomery GI bill enhancement act. Hearings Before the Subcommittee on Benefits of The Committee on Veterans Affairs, House of Representatives. One Hundredth Seventh Congress, First Session. Washington DC: House-HRG-107-6.

House Committee On Veterans' Affairs (2004). Subcommittee on health. Report of VA Advisory Committee on Homeless Veterans (PDF). Retrieved from http://veterans.house.gov/hearings/schedule108/may04/5-6-04/witness.html

Howell, T.   (2007). Report: Veteran homelessness on the rise. *Military.com.* September 12, 2007 from http://www.military.com/NewsContent/0,13319,139317,00.html

Huckabee, M. (2008) Congress Should First 'Bail Out' Our Veterans. FOX Forum.

Hunter, R. & Tankovich, M. B. (2007) The Army National Guard The You Can Guide to Paying for your College Education, 2nd Printing. Washington, D.C.: Uniformed Services Almanac, Inc. http://virtualarmory.com

Indiana Employer Support of the Guard and Reserve (INESGR) (2007) Investigations Provided to Indiana Higher Education to Service Members of the Guard and Reserve.

Indianapolis Healing Arts Program (2006). The Art of Combat Veterans: how visual and written arts may help people with PTSD and related disorders. Terre Haute, IN: Indiana State University.

Iraq and Afghanistan Veterans of America (IAVA) (2012) A survey of veterans about whether their college or university is veteran friendly. http:// chronicle.com/article/Veterans-Embrace-Post-9-11-GI/131318/

Iraq and Afghanistan Veterans of America (IAVA) (2011) Two urgent issues facing our community: 1) A threat to New GI Bill benefits 2) Some for-profit schools are exploiting loopholes in the federal law to make a buck.

Iraq and Afghanistan Veterans of America (IAVA) (2008a). A new GI Bill: Rewarding our troops, rebuilding our military. Issue report, January.

Iraq and Afghanistan Veterans of America (IAVA) (2008b). A new GI Bill: Rewarding our troops, rebuilding our military. Quick Facts, January.

JED (2010),"Voices of Vets".doc. www.HalfofUs.com. www.jedfoundation.org. Half of Us Support Our Veterans. Information on engaging with Veterans from Iraq and Afghanistan on college campuses and how you can support them with mental health issues facing Veterans, such as depression and suicide.

Jennings, P. A., Aldwin, C. M. Levenson, M. R., Spiro, A., & Mroczek, D. K. (2006). Combat Exposure, Perceived Benefits of Military Service, and Wisdom in Later Life: Findings From the Normative Aging Study. Research on Aging, 28, 115-134.

Joanning, H. (1975). The academic performance of Vietnam veteran college students. Journal of College Student Personnel, 16, 10-13.

91

Johnson, D. (2007).   College students protest Iraq War at Goshen College. Goshen Indiana: Goshen News.

Johnson, T. (2009). Ensuring the success of deploying students: A campus view. In Ackerman, R. & DiRamio, D. (Eds.), Creating aVeteran-Friendly Campus: Strategies for Transition and Success. New Directions for Student Services, No. 126, Jossey Bass: San Francisco.

Jones, D. (2005). Web extra: combat trains workplace leaders. Asbury & Park Press. . March 28. Retrieved on Jan 1, 2006 from http//www.app.com/apps/ pbcs.dll/article?AID=/20050328/BUSINESS/

Jowers, K. & Kauffman, T. (2007). Ruling strengthens vets' rights in federal job-bias claims. Army Times, 67, p25-25, 1/4p.

Judge, J. (2004). Where do soldiers come from? Washington Peace Letter. 40, (2), August/September . Retrieved Jan 15, 2006 from http:// www.washingtonpeacecenter.org/articles/0408pl.wheresoldiers.html

Keane, T. M. (1998). Psychological effects of military combat. *Adversity, Stress, and Psychopathology*, pp. 52-65. New York: Oxford University Press.

Kime, S. (2007a). Updating the Montgomery GI Bill. Committee on House Veterans Affairs Subcommittee on Economic Opportunity, 110th Congress. October 18.

Kime, S. (2007b). Why Veterans get Second-Class treatment. Retrieved from http://newscomet.com/

Kime, S. (2006). Transition assistance and educational benefits: Congressional testimony. Committee on House Veterans Affairs Subcommittee on Economic Opportunity. Congressional Quarterly, Inc., March 22.

Kime, S. F. (2005). Voluntary Military Education: A Strategic Perspective. Washington, D.C.: Servicemembers Opportunity Colleges.

Kingsbury, A. (2007). American Council on Education's new pilot program for wounded veterans. U.S. News & World Report. 143, 71-71.

Kingston, M. H. (2006). Veterans of War, Veterans of Peace. Kihei: Koa Books.

Klein, R. E. (1985). School enrollment among male veterans and non-veterans 20 to 34 years old. Washington, D. C.: Office of Information Management and Statistics.

Klimas, J. (2012)."Here's a college list we have faith in." Editorial – friendly and unfriendly colleges. Navy Times, April 23.

Kotok, A., (2008). Student Veterans Come Marching Home: Their Return to Studies, from: http://sciencecareers.sciencemag.org/career_development/previous_issues/articles/2008

Kramarow, E. A, % Pastor, P. N. (2012). The health of Male Veterans and Nonveterans aged 25-64: United States. National Center for Health Statistics Brief, No. 101, 1-5.

Kubany, E. S., Leisen, M. B., Kaplan, A. S. (2000). Development and preliminary validation of a brief broad-spectrum measure of trauma exposure. The Traumatic Life events questionnaire. Psychological Assessment. 12, 210-224.

Kubany, E. S., Haynes, S. N., & Abueg, F. R. (1996). Development and validation of the Trauma-Related Guilt Inventory(TRG). Psychological Assessment, 8, 428-444.

Labedz Poll, M. (2009) College forcing student out because she has service-related PTSD. University of Massachusetts, Boston,

Landau, E. (2002). Veterans Day: Remembering Our War Heroes. Berkeley Heights, NJ : Enslow Publishers.

Lane. C. (2005). Law Schools Challenge Rule Requiring Universities to Give Equal Access or Risk Losing Funding. Washington Post. May 3, Page A02.

Langbert, R., & Wells, W. (1982). Education and income characteristics of male war veterans and non-veterans. Washington, D. C.: Office of Reports and Statistics.

Lanham, S. L. (2005). Veterans and families guide to recovering from PTSD. Annandale, VA: Purple Heart Service Foundaion.

Lanigan, K. (2007). Operation education. VFW Magazine, September, 20-21.

Lavela, S. L., Weaver, F. M., Smith, B. & Chen, K. (2006). Disease Prevalence and Use of Preventive Services: Comparison of Female Veterans in General and Those with Spinal Cord Injuries and Disorders. Journal of Women's Health, 15, 301-311., 301-311.

Law Memo (2006). US Supreme Court unanimously upholds Solomon Amendment. March 06. from http://www.lawmemo.com/blog/2006/03/ us_supreme_cour_4.html

Lederman, D. (1997). Colleges That Bar the Military Won't Lose Most Student Aid. The Chronicle of Higher Education. : 02/21. Retrieved on September 22, 2007 from http: chronicle.com/che-data/articles.dir/art-43.dir/issue-24.dir/24a03401.htm - 20k - Cached - Similar pages - Note this

Leisner, B. A. (1995). Learning needs of hospitalized veteran patients: Developing a tool for practice. Patient Education and Counseling, 25, 151-162.

LeShan (1992). The Psychology of War: Comprehending its Mystique and its Madness. Chicago: Noble Press.

Leverenz, N. A. (2005). Not doing enough for our veterans. AlterNet. Retrieved on Jan 8, 2006 from http://alternet.org/story/27818/.

Lewin, T. (1990). Harvard Protesting R.O.T.C. Rejection Of Homosexuality. New York Times, June 15.

Lipka, S. (2011). Half of Student Veterans Have Contemplated Suicide, Study Shows. National Center for Veterans' Studies at the University of Utah and by Student Veterans of America. American Psychological Association, August National Meeting. Washington, D.C.

Lipsett, L. & Smith, L. F. (1949). Veterans carry through on operation "education." Journal of Educational Research, 42, 395-397.

Litz, B. T., Stein, N., Delaney, E., Lebowitz, L., Nash, W. P., Silva, C., Maguern, S. (2009) Moral injury and moral repair in war veterans: A preliminary model and Intervention Strategy. Clinical Psychology Review, Volume 29, Issue 8, 695–706.

Lokken, J. M. Pfeffer, D. S., McAuley, J. M. & Strong, C. (2009). A statewide approach to creating veteran-friendly campuses. In Ackerman, R. & DiRamio, D. (Eds.), Creating a Veteran-Friendly Campus: Strategies for Transition and Success. New Directions for Student Services, No. 126, Jossey Bass: San Francisco.

Maclean, A. (2005). Lessons from the cold war: Military service and college education. Sociology of Education, 78, 250.

Macias, W. (2010). Non-Tech Higher Education Rights. US Dept. of Education (Office of Postsecondary Education).

Maclean, L. & Roller , W. (2005). Students Protest Military Recruitment. The Golden Gate [Express] Online, San Francisco State University. March 9.

Madaus J. W. (2009). SPECIAL ISSUE: Veterans with Disabilities. Journal of Postseondary Education and Disabiity. AHEADAssociation, Volume 22, Number 1 • 2009 • Pages 1 – 74

Magruder, L. (2005). Turning their backs - again. Vietnam Veterans for Academic Reform. The University of Kansas Student Auxiliary. http://v-v-a-r.org/

Magruder, L. (2002). How the campus lied about vietnam. Vietnam Veterans for Academic Reform. The University of Kansas Student Auiliary. Retrieved on December 15 2006 from http://v-v-a-r.org/.

Majority Press (2010) Senate Hearing on Veterans' Access to Higher Education. The Senate Democratic Majority held a public hearing hosted by Senator Toby Ann Stavisky (Chairwoman of the Senate Higher Education   Committee) and Senator (Chair of the Senate Veterans, Homeland Security and Military Affairs Committee) . New York State Senate. from http:// www.nysenate.gov/press-release/senate-hearing-veterans-access-higher-education

Malladi, S. (2005). Students protest army presence. Badger Herald, University of Wisconsin Thursday, February 17, 2005

Malamud, O. & Wozniak, A. (2010). The Impact of College Education on Geographic Mobility: Identifying Education Using Multiple Components of Vietnam Draft Risk. college mobility and the Vietnam draft.

Malkin, M. (2008). It's time we quit coddling anti-military militants. Home News Tribune Online 03/13/08

Mangan, K. S. (2005). Affirmative Action and Military Recruiting Spur Debate at Law-School Meeting. Chronicle of Higher Education, pA19-A19.

Manguno-Mire, G., Sautter, F., Lyons, J., Myers, L., Perry, D., Sherman, M., Glynn, S., & Sullivan, M. (2007). Psychological Distress and Burden Among Female Partners of Combat Veterans With PTSD. Journal of Nervous and Mental Disease, 195, 144-151.

Marklein, M. B. (2007). Complex GI Bill makes for a rocky road from combat to college. USA TODAY, December 26.

Mason, P.H.D. (1990). Recovering from the war: A woman's guide to helping your Vietnam vet, your family, and yourself. New York: Penguin.

Massey, D. S. (2000). Higher Education and Social Mobility In the United States 1940-1998. Paper presented at the AAU Centennial Meeting, Washington D.C. April 17.

Maze, R. (2007b). Many hiring managers snubbing vets. *Federal Times*, 9/10/2007, Vol. 43 Issue 29, p1-20,

McDaniel, L. (2006). Campus Veterans Clubs Boost Camaraderie and Careers. VFW Magazine, 25 Jan. Retrieved on January 15, 2008 from https:// www.vfw.org/inde.cfm?fa=news.magDt&dtl=2&mid=2148>.

McBain, L. (2008). When Johnny [or Janelle] comes marching home: National, state, and institutional efforts in support of veteran's education. Perspectives: American Association of State Colleges and Universities, Summer Issue.

McCaffrey, N. (2011) Eli Painted Crow/Cpt. Anu Bhagwati.to Columbia University School of Social Work. Taken from McCaffrey's Facebook page. See also: anu@servicewomen.org "brad@lunamediagroup.com", "John DMikelson" <john-mikelson@uiowa.edu>

McDaniel, L. (2006). Campus Veterans Clubs Boost Camaraderie and Careers. VFW Magazine, 25 Jan. Retrieved on January 15, 2008 from

McGrevey, M. & Keher, D. (2009) Stewards of the public trust: Federal laws that serve service members and student veterans. In Ackerman, R. & DiRamio, D. (Eds.), Creating a Veteran-Friendly Campus: Strategies for Transition and Success. New Directions for Student Services, No. 126, Jossey Bass: San Francisco.

McLay, R. N. & Lyketsos, C. G. (2000). Veterans have less age related cognitive decline. Military Medicine, 165, 622-625.

Mears, B. (2005). Pentagon, law schools square off. CNN News. 6 Dec. 2005. Retrieved on January 5, 2006 from http://www.cnn.com/2005/LAW/12/06/scotus/recruiters/. http://www.cnn.com/TECH/computing/9905/28/vets.idg/

Mehrabian, A. (1969).   Significance of posture and position in the communication of attitude and status relationships. *Psychological Bulletin, 71*, 359-392.

Mettler, S. (2005). Soldiers to citizens: The GI Bill and the Making of the Greatest Generation. Cambridge: Oxford Univ. Press.

Milliken, C.S., Auchterlonie, J.L., & Hoge, C.W. (November 14, 2007). Longitudinal Assessment of Mental Health Problems among Active and Reserve Component Solders Returning from the Iraq War. JAMA, 298 (18), 2141-2148.

Minnesota State Colleges and Universities (2008) Health and health related behaviors: Minnesota Postsecondary Student Veterans. Boyton Health Service.

Mindy, A., & Lester, D. (1994). Attitudes toward war in veterans. Psychological Reports, 75, 314.

Minnesota Online Veterans (2007). Retrieved on March 21 2007 from http:// www.acenet.edu/AM/Template.cfm?Section=For_the_Record&Template

Minnesota National Guard (2007a) Family readiness programs that include information on going to college. See http://www.minnesotanationalguard.org/education

Minnesota National Guard (2007b). A Family Reintegration Program. Retrieved on Septermber 28th, 2007 from http://www.minnesotanationalguard.org/ returning_troops/btyr_overview.php -

Mullane, L. (2005). Soldiers and scholars: what the military and higher education can teach each other. The American Council on Education. Retrieved on September 1, 2007 from http://www.acenet.edu/AM/Template.cfm? Section=Search&template=/CM/HTMLDisplay.cfm&ContentID=11193.

Muran, E. M., & Motta, R. W. (1993). Cognitive distortions and irrational beliefs in post-traumatic stress, anxiety, and depressive disorders. Journal of Clinical Psychology, 49, 166-176.

Murphy, E. (2011) Operation Graduation. Inside higher ed. November.

Murphy, M. M. (2011). Military Veterans and College Success. University of North Carolina, Greensboro.

National Center for Education Statistics (2011). Military Service Members and Veterans: A Profile of Those Enrolled in Undergraduate and Graduate Education in 2007–08.

National Coalition for Homeless Veterans. (2007). Facts and media. Retrieved on September 12, 2007 from http://www.nchv.org/background.cfm National Guard Family Program (2003). Staying Together. www.guardfamily.org See also www.lifeskillsused.com

National Guard Family Program (2003). Staying Together. www.guardfamily.org See also www.lifeskillsused.com

National Resource Directory (2010). Programs and services for veterans at a national, state, and local level. https://www.nationalresourcedirectory.gov/clickTrack/ confirm/13881177?external=true&parentFolderId=39334&linkId=365894

NAVPA (2006). National association of veterans ' program administrators. Retrieved on March 21 2007 from http://www.navpa.org/web_membership.htm - 26k - Cached –Similarpages.

NAVREF. (2006). National association of veterans' research and education foundation. Retrieved on March 21, 2007 from http://www.navref.org/ - 14k - Cached –Similar pages

National Veterans Foundation (2007). Home Page: Veterans helping veterans. Retrieved on March 22, 2007 from http://www.nvf.org/?q=

National Veterans Legal Services Program (2007). Veterans Benefit Manual. Retrieved on October 24, 2007 from http://www.nvlsp.org/Information/inde.ht

National Veterans Training Institute (1994). The resource center: helping build your information network. Denver, Colorado: U. S. Department of Labor.

Nelson, L. (2012). GI Bill TM. Inside Higher Ed. From http://www.insidehighered.com/news/2012/04/27/obama-issues-executive-order- veterans-recruiting#ixzz28cOQGTS7

Nelson, S. S. (2006). Governor wants more veterans in state's colleges. The Orange County Register.

Neuts, D. (2011). Are dual relationships on campus placing veterans in harms way. Universities 101. Read more at Suite101: Are Dual Relationships On Campus Placing Veterans in Harms Way? From http://www.suite101.com/content/are-dual-relationships-on-campus-placing-veterans-in- harms-way-a363127#ixzz1IHZGANjSs

Next Student (2007). American Council on Education Meeting: Questions on Accountability. 13 February.. www.nextstudent.com.

Nilsen, W. R. (2001) Veterans' Employment and Training Service: Flexibility and accountability needed to improve service to veterans. Report to the Chairman, Subcommittee on Oversight and Investigations, Committee on Veterans' Affairs, House of Representatives. Washington DC: General Accounting Office (GAO-01-928)

North, O. (2005) [Anti] Military Operations. Freedom Alliance, July 21. http: www.military.com/Opinions/0,,FreedomAlliance_072105,00.html - 37k –

North Carolina University (2007). Seminars on seminars on how veterans are a protected class. From
http://www.ncsu.edu/equal_op/education/oeo_programs.html).

Nursing Standard (2007). Men who have served in the armed forces at high risk of suicide. Nursing Standard, 21, p17-17.
http://www.nursing-standard.co.uk/inde.asp

O'Donnell, M. A. (2002). The G.I. bill of rights of 1944 and the creation of America's modern middle class society. New York: St. John's University.

Office of Academic Affiliations (2005). General military service history. Retrieved from
http://www.vba,va.gov/oaa/pocketcard.

Olson, K. (1974). The G.I. bill, the veterans, and the colleges. Lexington, Kentucky.

Paige, C. (2007). Home from America's wars, yet homeless in its suburbs. The Boston Globe. September 14, 2007 from http://www.boston.com/news/local/articles/ 2007/08/12/home_from_americas_wars_yet_homeless_in_its_suburbs/

Parade (2008). The fight for ROTC. November 30th.

Partnership for veterans education (2006). Retrieved on March 15, 2007 from http:veterans.house.gov/hearings/schedule109/sep06/9-27 06a/NorbertRyan.html - 36k

Pathway Home (2007). Pathway home for the Care of Combat Veterans. Retrieved on January 19, 2009 from http://www.va.gov/OPA/fact/returning_vets.asp..

Patraeus, H. K. (2011). For-Profit Colleges, Vulnerable G.I.'s. Opinion Pages: New York Times. September.

Paul, R. (2003)   Mistreating Soldiers and Veterans. Ron Paul Archives. Member of Congress from Texas.

Paulson, A. (2010). Veterans Day survey: 300,000 use revamped GI Bill. Christian Science Monitor. November 10.

Penn Foster College (2007) A complaint about transfer credits. Home web site. Retrieved from
http://www.pennfostercollege.edu/inde.html?semkey=Q092370

Penn State (2009) "worrisome student behaviors vets.doc." POSTED AT 8:28 PM ON APRIL 7, 2009 BY ALLAHPUNDIT.
http://hotair.com/archives/2009/04/07/video-psychotically-angry-military-veterans-and-the-academics-who-must-tolerate-them/

Penzenstadler, N. (2007) Students (from the University of Wisconsin at Madison) join D.C. war protest. The Badger Herald, University of Wisconsin.

Peter, H. M. (1975). Effects of open admission on the academic adjustment of Vietnam veterans. Journal of College Student Personnel, 16, pp 14-16.

Peterson's College Planner (2007a). National Call to Service and Education Benefits: GI Bill Education Benefits. A Nelnet Company. All Rights Reserved. Retrieved from http://www.petersons.com/common/article.asp? id=1667&path=ug.pfs.advice&sponsor=1

Peterson's College Planner (2007b). Did You Know? Free Information Article: College Education for Veterans. Retrieved from http://www.petersons.com/

Petrovic, K. (2006). Anti-military sentiments persist on elite campus. VFW.

Pierre, R. E (2003) Students Across U.S. Mount Antiwar Protests. Published on Thursday, March 6, Washington Post

Pope, J. (2012). "Military friendly' college lists may be misleading. Navy Times, April 23.

Portnoy (2008) Working with returning veterans, and other non-traditional students. UNMC, power point. November 7.

Post 9/11 (2009) Veterans Education Assistance Act (Chapter 33). This act was signed into law on June 30, 2008 and will take effect August 1, 2009. http://www.gibill.va.gov/S22/Post 911

Powell, G. J., & Doan, R. E. (1992). Combat and social support as variables in perceived symptomatology of combat-related post traumatic stress disorder. *Psychological Reports, 70*, 1187-1194.

Price, C. W. (1980). Preliminary study of the scholastic progress of veteran with honorable and general discharges. Psychological Reports, 47, 1174.

Pryor, J. H. Hurtado, S. DeAngelo, L., Palucki Blake, L., & Tran, S. (2009), The American Freshman: National Norms Fall 2009. The Cooperative Institutional Research Program (CIRP) Higher Education Research Institute, UCLA. From http://www.heri.ucla.edu.

Quillen-Armstrong, S. (2007). Course to help transition veterans into civilian life. July 5., Community College Times Web site: Retrieved on July 16, 2007 from http://www.communitycollegetimes.com/article.cfm?Article, Id=417

Radford, A. W. and Wun, J. (2009). Issues tables: A Profile of military servicemembers and veterans enrolled in post-secondary education from 2008-9. Retrieved December 15, 2009, from http://nces.ed.gov/pubs2009/2009182.pdf

Rentz, E. D., Martin, S. L., Gibbs, D. A., Clinton-Sherrod, M., Hardison, J. & Marshall, S. W.. (2006). Family Violence in the Military: A Review of the Literature. Trauma, Violence, & Abuse, 7, 93-108.

Reston, J. (1997). Education programs available to enlisted personnel and veterans. Black Issues in Higher Education, *14*, 38-42.

Rieckhoff, P. (2011). A threat to New GI Bill benefits. Iraq and Afghanistan Veterans of America (IAVA).

Roca, V. & Freeman, T. W. (2001). Complaints of impaired memory in veterans with PTSD. American Journal of Psychiatry, 158, 1738-1739.

Roche, J. (2000). The Veteran's Survival Guide: How to File and Collect on VA Claims. Washington, D.C.: Brassey's Incs.

Rollins, P. C. (1993) Behind the Westmoreland Trial of 1984. Journal of the Vietnam Veterans Institute, 2, No. 1.

Rosenzweig, Y. (2002). Harvard joins national anti-war protest. The Record, Harvard Law Journal, Issue date: 10/10/02 Section: News.

Ross, D. B. (1969). Preparing for Ulysses: politics and veterans during World War II. NewYork.: Columbia University Press

Roth-Douquet, K. & Schaeffer, F. (2007). "AWOL: The Unexcused Absence of America's Upper Classes from Military Service—and How It Hurts Our Country," New York: Collins.

Roth-Douquet, K. & Schaeffer, F. (2006b). Those who serve. Blueprint, 2, 16-20.

Rumann, C. B. & Hamrick, F. A. (2009) Supporting student veterans in Transition. In Ackerman, R. & DiRamio, D. (Eds.) Creating a Veteran-Friendly Campus: Strategies for Transition and Success. New Directions for Student Services, No. 126, Jossey Bass: San Francisco.

Ryan, H. P. (2009). Hank Investigates: Veterans' Problems. 7 PM News NBC. October.

Sailer, S. (2004). Comparison of IQ of Veterans and nonveterans by State. Sailer Archives. Retrieved on August 8, 2006 from http://www.vdare.com/sailer/inde.htm

Schlachter, G. A. (1998). Financial Aid for Veterans, Military Personnel and Their Dependents, 1998-2000. Redwood City, CA: Reference Service Press. Eric # ED291315

Schnurr, P. P., Rosenberg, S. D., & Friedman, M. J. (1993). Change in MMPI scores from college to adulthood as a function of military service. Journal of Abnormal Psychology, *150*, 479-483.

Schram, M. (2008) Veterans under siege: How America Deceives and dishonors those who fight our battles. New York: St. Martins. Retrieved on September 14 from http://www.veteransforamerica.org/home/vfa/

Serow, R. C. (2004). Policy as symbol: title ii of the 1944 GI Bill. Review of Higher Education. 27, 481.

Servicemembers Opportunity Colleges. (2004). What is SOC? Retrieved on February 5, 2005, from http://www.soc.aascu.org/socgen/WhatIs.html.

Severo, R. & Milford, L. (1990). The Wages of War: When America's soldiers came home – from Valley Forge to Vietnam. New York: Touchstone.

Servicemembers Opportunity Colleges (SOC). (2007a). Retrieved on Aug 25, 2007 from
http://www.soc.aascu.org/

Servicemembers Opportunity Colleges (2007b). Veterans Education Bill of Rights. Presented to the Veterans Affairs Committee on Education, May 16.

Servicemembers Opportunity Colleges. (2004). What is SOC? Retrieved February 5, 2004, from http://www.soc.aascu.org/socgen/WhatIs.html.

Shepard, B. (2003). A war of nerves: Soldiers and psychiatrist in the twentieth century. Cambridge: Harvard University Press.

Sherman, M. D., Zanotti, D. K. & Jones, D. E. (2005). Key Elements in Couples Therapy With Veterans With Combat-Related Posttraumatic Stress Disorder. Professional Psychology: Research and Practice, 36, 626-633

Shuckra, D. (2006). Retaining adult learners: what works? The American Council on Education. September 3, 2007 from http://www.acenet.edu/AM/ Template.cfm?Section=Search&template=/CM/HTMLDisplay.cfm&ContentID=22087.

Sinner, C. (2008) 16 arrested in anti-war protest; More than 200 protesters joined in the march around the University campus Thursday. Macalester College Minnesota Daily, University of Minnesota, Minneapolis.

Snyder, L. B. (2002). Cashing in on the G.I. Billl. Soldiers. 57, 22.

Sparta/Gannett, S. (2008). Rutgers students march on Route 18, down N street. Rutgers University, New Brunswick, New Jersey.

Spaulding Ç, D. J., Eddy, J. P., Chandras, K. V. (1997). Gulf war syndrome: Are campus health officials prepared to cope with Persian Gulf veterans. College Student Journal, 31, 317-322.

Stand Down (2007). Stand Down for Homeless Veterans. Retrieved from http://www.navy.mil/search/display.asp?story id=3061

Stanley, M. (2003). Policy as Symbol: Title II of the 1944 G.I. Bill. Quarterly Journal of Economics. Cambridge: May 2003. 118, Issue. 2; p. 671.

State of Illinois (2011). Higher Education Veterans Services Act: Services and Programs for Veterans, Military Personnel, and their Families at Public Colleges and Universities. From
http://www.ibhe.state.il.us/Veteran/List.asp

Steigmeyer, R. (2009, February 21) From combat to college: A tough transition that few understand. Wenatchee World. Retrieved from http:// wenatcheeworld.com/article/20090221/NEWS04/702219970

Sternberg, M., MacDermid Wadsworth, S., Vaughan, J., & Carlson, R. (2009). The higher education landscape for student service members and veterans in Indiana. West Lafayette: Military Family Research Institute at Purdue.

Stever, J. A. (1996). The veteran and the neo-progressive campus. Academic Questions, 10, 41-52.

Stiglitz, J. E. & Bilmes, L. J. (2008) The Three Trillion Dollar War: The True Cost of the Iraq Conflict. New York: Norton, W. W. & Company.

Storzbach, D., Campbell, K. A., Binder, L. M., McCauley, L., Anger, W., K., Rohlmann, & D. S., Kovera, C. A. (2000). Psychological differences between veterans with and without gulf war unexplained symptoms. Psychosomatic Medicine, 62, 726-735

Straus, R. (2005). Vet-to-vet counseling heals new and old soldiers. Columbia News Service, Nov 1.

Students for a Democratic Society (SDS) (2008). Press release anti Iraq in schools around the nation. Retrieved April 8, 2008

Sullivan, K., Krengel, M., Proctor, S. P., Devine, S., Heeren, T. & White, R. F. (2003). Cognitive functioning in treatment-seeking gulf war veterans: pyridostigmine bromine use and PTSD. Journal of Psychopathology & Behavioral Assessment, 25, 95-103.

Summerlot, J., Green, S.M. (2009). Student veterans organizations. In Ackerman, R. & DiRamio, D. (Eds.) Creating a Veteran-Friendly Campus: Strategies for Transition and Success. New Directions for Student Services, No. 126, Jossey Bass: San Francisco.

Tapp, D. (2009) Veteran's mistreatment: loss of freedom. Maricopa County Libertarian Examiner, November 10.

Teachman, J, (2005). Military service in the Vietnam era and educational attainment. Sociology of Education, 78, 50.

Thirtle, R. M. (2001). Educational benefits and officer-commissioning opportunities available to U.S. military servicemembers. Santa Monica, CA: RAND Corporation. Available at
http://www.rand.org/publications/MR/MR981

Thompson, J. (1997) Teaching the Vietnam War to Generation X. Journal of the Vietnam Veterans Institute, 6, No. 1-4.

Thomson, M. (2011). The other 1%. Nation, Time Magazine, November, 33-41.

Thorn, R. G. & Payne, S. L. (1977). Ethical judgments of armed service veterans attending college. Psychological Reports, 41, 337-338.

Tick, E. (2005). War and the Soul Healing our Nations Veterans from Post-traumatic Stress Disorder. Wheaton, Ill: Theosophical Publishing House.

Tiet, Q., Finney, J., & Moos, R. H. (2006). Recent sexual abuse, physical abuse, and suicide attempts among male veterans seeking psychiatric treatment. Psychiatric Services, 57, 107-113.

Todd, W. E. (1949). Rehabilitation and education for veterans of World War II. Stanford University Bulletin, Abstracts of Dissertations, ser 8(35).

Totenberg (2011). Troops, Vets Find Vindication On The Supreme Court. http://www.npr.org/2011/03/01/134177095/Supreme-Court-Rules-In-Favor-Of-Military-Personnel?sc=emaf

Traina, T. (2004). Appeals court rules colleges can ban recruiters from campuses. Heretical Ideas.com. Retrieved on October 8 from http:hereticalideas.com/?p=2582 - 25k - Cached - Similar pages - Note this

Trewyn, R.W. (1994). Discrimination Against Veterans by the Federal Agency Charged With Protecting Veterans' Rights. Journal of the Vietnam Veterans Institute, 3, 22-36.

Trewyn, R. A. & Stever, J. A. (1995). Academia: Not So hallowed halls for veterans. Journal of the Vietnam Veterans Institute, 4, 63-75.

Tucker, J. (2006). War of nerves: Chemical welfare from World War I to al-Qaeda. Cambridge: Harvard University Press.

UKentucky (2010) "Civilian" a theater about Iraq vets: University of Kentucky Students Find Unique Way to Honor Veterans. www.youtube.com/watch? v=Fd7Ut84Ut2sNov10, 2010 - 4 min - Uploaded by Universityofkentucky.

UMKC Institute for Human Development (2011). Transition STEM: A Wounded Warriors Think Tank. KC BANCS. University of Oregon Counseling Center (2009). Issues Faced when Transitioning to Campus.

U.S. Census Bureau (2003). U.S. armed forces and veterans. U.S. Census Bureau, Public Information Office. Special Edition. Retrieved Jun 1, 2004 from http://www.census.gov/prod/2003pubs/02statab/defense.pdf.

U.S. Census Bureau (2001). Current population survey. Publication Office. Retrieved Jun 1, 2004 from http://www.census.gov.

U.S. Census Bureau (2000). The graduates: Educational attainment. Retrieved Jun 1, 2004 from http://www.census.gov/prod/2003pubs/02statab/defense.pdf.

U.S. Department of Education (2009). U.S. Department of Education Database of Accredited Postsecondary Institutions and Programs. Retrieved November 10, 2009, from http://ope.ed.gov/accreditation/

U.S. Department of Labor (2011). "US Department of Labor re-launches National Resource Directory for wounded warriors with US Departments of Defense and Veterans Affairs." Retrieved 18 March 2011.

U.S. Department of Veterans Affairs (2004). EEO progress report. Retrieved from   http://www.google.com/search?hl=en&q=U.S.+Department+of +Veterans+Affairs+%282004%29&btnG=Search

US Fed News Service, Including US State News. (2007) Webb (D-VA) l introducing a sweeping expansion of the education. Washington, D.C.: Jan 4.

Vacchi, D. (2012) Veteran's Knowledge. NASPA National Veterans Knowledge Community.

Van Devanter, L & J.A. Furey., Eds., (1991). Visions of War, Dreams of Peace: Writings of women in the Vietnam War. Warner, New York.

Veterans Administration (2006a). A Brief History of the VA. Office of Construction & Facilities Retrieved on January 15, 2007 from   http:www.va.gov/ facmgt/historic/Brief_VA_History.asp - 19k

Veterans Administration (2006b). History of the Department of Veterans Affairs. Retrieved on January 15, 2007 from http: www.va.gov/facmgt/historic/Brief_VA_History.asp - 19k

Veterans Administration. (1991). Federal benefits for veterans and dependents. Washington, D. C.: Veterans Administration.

Veterans Committee On Education (2007) Problems of Vets in college." What It is Like to Be a Veteran in College Today. Veterans Education Association, Terre Haute.

Veterans Education Association (2008) Vets college problems: Practices of Some Higher Educational Institutions in America that Discourage Veterans from Obtaining a College Degree. power point.

Veterans for America (2008) About veterans for America. Retrieved on November 22 from http://www.veteransforamerica.org/home/vfa/

Veterans Information Service (2003). *What every veteran should know.* East Moline, Ill: Library of Congress. s

Veterans Museum & Memorial (2004). Retrieved from http:// www.veteranmuseum.org/

Vietnam Era Veterans Readjustment Assistance Act (1974); Title 38 United States Code Section 4212.

Vincennes University (2008) Military Education Program Handbook: Arkansas Edition. Vincennes, Indiana 47591 from www.vinu.edu/military

Walker, C. (2010) Vet barred from campus for essay on killing. The Baltimore Sun, November 24. 2010. From http://voices.washingtonpost.com/collegeinc/2011/01/ iraq_vet_exits_ccbc_over_essy.html http://www.insidehighered.com/news/2010/11/23/

Walters, A. K. (2006). State contributions to veterans education benefits. Chronicle of Higher Education, 52, 18.

Webb, J. (2007). Introducing a sweeping expansion of the education. US Fed News Service, Including US State News. Washington, D.C.: Jan 4.

Wector, D. (1944). When Johnny comes marching home. Boston: Houghton Mifflin.

Weingartner, N. (2008). Disabled Veterans Returning From Iraq and Afghanistan Face Problems With Education. Digital Journal. May.

Wenger, D., Rufflo, M., & Bertalan, F. J. (2006). ACME project, internet-based systems that advocate VA credit for military experience and analyze options for veterans in career transition. Proceedings of the IEEE International Conference on Advanced Learning Techniques, IEEE The Computer Society.

Wilkes-Edrington, L (2007). First battle: serve in military. Net battle: finish college. The Missourian. Retrieved on September 14 2007 from http://www.columbiamissourian.com/stories/2007/05/26/first-battle-serve-military-net-battle-finish-col/

Williams,K. & Rochelson, J. (2010). Veterans talk transition to college The Michigan Daily. November 16, 2010.

Williamson, V. (2008) A New GI Bill: Rewarding our Troops, Rebuilding our Military. Iraq and Afghanistan Veterans of America, issue report.

Winter, G. (2005). From Combat To Campus On the G.I. Bill. New York Times (Late Edition (East Coast)). New York, N.Y.: Jan 16,p. 4A.8

Wilson, R. (2006). Professor Charges Bias Over War Injuries. Chronicle of Higher Education; 9/1/2006, 53, 2, 23-23.

Wilson, R. B. (2003). Indiana State University's Veterans Handbook. Terre Haute, IN: Indiana University Press.

Winter, G. (2005). From Combat To Campus On the G.I. Bill. New York Times (Late Edition (East Coast)). New York, N.Y.: Jan 16,p. 4A.8

Wisconsin Department of Veterans Affairs (2007). Wisconsin G.I. Bill Tuition Remission Program. Retrieved on October 24 from http://dva.state.wi.us/Ben_education.asp

Yates, J. E. (1993). Hello Miss American Pie (An essay for Veterans Day, 1992). Journal of the Vietnam Veterans Institute, 2, No. 1.

Yates, J. (2004) Examining the myths of the Vietnam War. A conference held at Simmons College by the RADIX Foundation, Journal of the Vietnam Veterans Institute, 26-29 July.

Yehuda, R., Keefe, R. S. E., & Harvey, P. D. , Levengood, R. A., et al. (1995). Learning and memory in combat veterans with posttraumatic stress disorder. American Journal of Psychiatry, 152, 137-139.

Young, A. (2005). Bureaucratic tangle delays education payments to veterans. Knight Ridder/Tribune News Service. November 1.

YouTube (2003). Anti war protest of college students in Austin, Texas.

Zahn, P. (2007). Epidemic of mental illness in U.S.. military? War and women. Paula Zahn Now. Retrieved Dec 3, 2007 from http://panther.indstate.edu:2048/login?url=http://panther.indstate.edu:2920/login.asp?direct=true&db=nfh&AN=32U0942688305CNPZ&site=ehost-live.

Zimmerman, J. (2007). The Liberal (and Moderating) Professoriate. Inside Higher Ed, October 8.

B(3) – [4] Articles Reporting Surveys of veterans and/or educators About How Veterans Cope with Abuse while Seeking a College Degree. Concern about abuse of student veterans has grown over the past decade. Several surveys have assessed the extent of this abuse.

Ackerman, R., & DiRamio, D. (2008). From combat to campus: Voices of student-veterans. NASPA Journal, 45(1), 73-94.

Cook, B. J. & Kim, Y. (2008) From Soldier to Student: Easing the Transition of Service Members on Campus. Lumina Foundation. [A survey investigation of colleges; Statistics of college services for veterans].

Fiore, S.M. & da Costa da Silveira, A. (2010) Curriculum and Culture: A Preliminary Look at the Experiences of Veterans in Higher Education.

Herrmann (2007) Investigations into Services of Indiana Higher Education to Members of the of Guard and Reservists. Veterans Higher Education Group. Terre Haute, Indiana.

Herrmann, D. (2010). Indiana's Best Practices for the Higher Education of Servicemembers and Veterans. Veterans Higher Education Group. Terre Haute, Indiana.

Iraq and Afghanistan of America (IAVA) (2012) A survey of veterans about whether their college or university is veteran friendly. http://chronicle.com/article/Veterans-Embrace-Post-9-11-GI/131318/

Liker, S. (2011). Half of Student Veterans Have Contemplated Suicide, Study Shows. National Center for Veterans' Studies at the University of Utah and by Student Veterans of America. American Psychological Association, August: National Meeting.

Lipka, S. (2011). Half of Student Veterans Have Contemplated Suicide, Study Shows. National Center for Veterans' Studies at the University of Utah and by Student Veterans of America. American Psychological Association, August National Meeting. Washington, D.C.

Minnesota State Colleges and Universities (2008) HEALTH AND HEALTH-RELATED BEHAVIORS survey: Minnesota Postsecondary Student Veterans. Boyton Health Service.

National Survey of Student Engagement (NSSE)(2010). Annual results. www. nsse . iub. edu.

Pryor, J. H. Hurtado, S. DeAngelo, L., Palucki Blake, L., & Tran, S. (2009), The American Freshman: National Norms Fall 2009. The Cooperative Institutional Research Program (CIRP) Higher Education Research Institute, UCLA. www.heri.ucla.edu.

Radford, A. W. (2009). Military Service Members and Veterans in Higher Education: What the New GI Bill May Mean for Postsecondary Institutions. American Council on Education. Washington, D.C.

Smith, W. (2010). Missouri College Health Behavior Survey. contact Joan Masters at mastersj@missouri.edu or (573) 884-755

Sternberg, M., MacDermid Wadsworth, S., Vaughan, J., & Carlson, R. (2009). The higher education landscape for student service members and veterans in Indiana. West Lafayette: Military Family Research Institute at Purdue.

Vance, M. L. & Miller, W. K. & Wayne K. (2009). Special Issue: Veterans with Disabilities, J. W. Madaus (special issue editor). Serving Wounded Warriors: Current Practices in Postsecondary Education (A nationwide survey of members of the Association on Higher Education and Disability (AHEAD).). Journal of Postsecondary Education and Disability, Vol. 22, No. 1; 2009.

Veterans Success Jam (2010). American Council on Education, Washington, D.C.

Winter, G. (2005). From Combat To Campus On the G.I. Bill. New York Times (Late Edition (East Coast)). New York, N.Y.: Jan 16,p. 4A.8

References for Chapter 4 concerning information about how particular schools abuse veterans

Ackerman, R. & DiRamio, D. (Eds.) (2009). In Creating a Veteran-Friendly Campus: Strategies for Transition and Success New Directions for Student Services, No. 126, Wiley Periodicals.

College Educators for Veterans Higher Education (2009). How to Improve the College Education of Veterans. A conference held at SOC headquarters in October 2009.

Cook, B. J., & Kim. Y. (2009). From Soldier to Student: Easing the Transition of Service Members on Campus. Lumina Foundation.

Georgetown University Conference (2009). How to improve education of veterans at Georgetown University – October 2009.

Hopkins, C., Herrmann, D. J., Wilson, R. B., Allen, B., & Malley, L. (Eds.) (2010). Improving College Education of Veterans. North Charleston, South Carolina: Create Space.

Indiana Employer Support of the Guard and Reserve (2007). Indiana Symposium on the Higher Education of Guard Members and Reservists, September.

Lipka, S. (2011). Half of Student Veterans Have Contemplated Suicide, Study Shows. National Center for Veterans' Studies at the University of Utah and by Student Veterans of America. American Psychological Association, August: National Meeting. Washington, D.C.

Penn State (2009) training video, "worrisome student behaviors vets.doc." POSTED AT 8:28 PM ON APRIL 7, 2009 BY ALLAHPUNDIT. http://hotair.com/ archives/2009/04/07/video-psychotically-angry-military-veterans-and-the-academics-who-must-tolerate-them/

Smith, W. (2010). Missouri College Health Behavior Survey. contact Joan Masters at mastersj@missouri.edu or (573) 884-755

Sternberg, M., MacDermid Wadsworth, S., Vaughan, J., & Carlson, R. (2009). The higher education landscape for student service members and veterans in Indiana. West Lafayette: Military Family Research Institute at Purdue.

References for Chapter 5 concerning why professors and administrators abuse veterans

Brown, W. (2011) Veterans For Education. Brian Teter Disabled vet kicked out of college. Iraqi war veteran claims discrimination. http://video.foxnews.com/v/ 1181448445001/disabled-vet-kicked-out-of-college/?playlist_id=86856

Cook, B. J., & Kim. Y. (2009). From Soldier to Student: Easing the Transition of Service Members on Campus. Lumina Foundation.

Clark, D. A. (1998). "The Two Joes meet – Joe College and Joe Veteran:" The GI Bill, College Education, and Postwar American Culture. History of Education Quarterly, Vol. 38, No, 2, 165-189.

Fontana, A. & Rosenhack, R. (2004). Trauma, change in strength of religious faiths, and mental health service use among veterans treated for PTSD. Journal of Nervous and Mental Diseases, Vol. 192, Sept, 579-584.

Frederiksen, N. (1951). Adjustment to College: A study of 10,000 Veteran and Nonveteran Students in Sixteen American Colleges. Educational Testing Service: Princeton, NJ.

Herrmann, D. J., Hopkins, C., Wilson, R. B., & Allen, B. (2011). Progress in educating veterans in the 21st Century. North Charleston, South Carolina: Create Space.

Herrmann, D. J., Hopkins, C., Wilson, R. B., & Allen, B. (2009). Educating veterans in the 21st Century. North Charleston, South Carolina: BookSurge.

Hopkins, C., Herrmann, D. J., Wilson, R. B., Allen, B., & Malley, L. (Eds.) (2010). Improving College Education of Veterans. North Charleston, South Carolina: Create Space.

Madaus, J. W. (2009). SPECIAL ISSUE: Veterans with Disabilities. Journal of Postseondary Education and Disability. AHEAD Association, Volume 22, Number 1 • 2009 • Pages 1 – 74

Penn State (2009) "worrisome student behaviors vets.doc." POSTED AT 8:28 PM ON APRIL 7, 2009 BY ALLAHPUNDIT.

Sternberg, M., MacDermid Wadsworth, S., Vaughan, J., & Carlson, R. (2009). The higher education landscape for student service members and veterans in Indiana. West Lafayette: Military Family Research Institute at Purdue.

References for Chapter 6 concerning writings about ways to encourage professors and administrators to treat veterans fairly.

I[1]. Federal Programs, I[2]. Corporate Programs, I [3]. State Programs

I[1]. Federal Programs intended to ensure that servicemembers and veterans are treated properly as they seek a college degree

a. Servicemembers Opportunity Colleges (SOC) – college and university members promise to treat service members and veterans fairly as they seek a college degree.

b. Veterans Centers established around the country after the Vietnam War to deal with personal problems and in those cases that a veteran decided to go to college.

c. Transfer credit laws. Since 1945, the American Council on Education (ACE) has enabled higher educational institutions to give veterans and service members transfer credits for their military training and military experience

d. In his State of the Union address in 2011 President Obama acknowledged that some members of higher education treated veterans negatively; he enjoined colleges and universities to allow recruiters and ROTC programs back on campus.

e. In an Executive Order, set forth on April 27, 2012, President Obama provided legal restrictions on higher educations abuse of veterans.

f. Post-9/11 GI Bill for School Certifying Officials, Veterans Education Assistance Improvements Act of 2010, will affect schools, certifying officials and students.

g. VA National Directory. This web site provides information on education and job training opportunities including scholarships, tuition assistance programs, the GI Bill, the Yellow Ribbon Program and more. The directory discusses several sources of help to educators and to service members/veterans in college.

      (1) Information is provided on the academic challenges encountered by student Veterans with TBI and PTSD face.

      (2) The Council of College and Military Educators facilitates communication between the organization's members and the DoD educational support network.

(3) From Soldier to Student eases the Transition of
Service Members and veterans on Campus by
explaining college programs, services and
policies.

(4) The American Council on Education reviews
military training and experiences that qualify for
college credits for members of the Armed Forces.

(5) Data on service members and veterans already
enrolled in higher education are presented to help
higher education administrators anticipate
the enrollment choices of returning veterans and
military personnel under the new GI Bill.

(6) The American Council on Education. Provides
information and   resources on how to make a
higher education institution suitable for Veterans.

(7) Student Veterans organizations discuss programs to
help student Veterans in college.

I[2]. Corporate Programs
Writings of some corporate programs are intended to help veterans avoid
higher educational abuse. Some businesses make money by providing
information to veterans about colleges to attend and on how to cope
with unfriendly practices at a college and to educators about their
practices. These corporations include:

(a) Walmart and American Council on Education;
(b) Lilly: Operation Diploma
(c) Businesses can offer Web courses to professors and/or
college administrators about veterans in higher
education: Innovative Educators, 2010; help to
vets find employment (VetJobs, 2010;
Military.Com].

I[3]. State Government programs to prevent educational abuse of
veterans.

(a). The University of Illinois changed admission
sprocedures in July of 2009 to keep military
veterans out of Illinois colleges.

(b). Indiana Military Families Relief Act.pdf

(c). New Vet Ed from VA ed benefits 11 2011

(d). Best Practices, Servicemembers Vet Students, Indiana
Hi Ed 12 2 08.doc

(e). OHIO GI Promise Fact Sheet.pdf

(f). Illinois (2011). Higher Education Veterans Services Act.
(P.A. 96-0133). The act requires all public colleges
and universities to conduct a survey of the services
and programs that are provided for their families.
Retrieved from
http://Illinois hi ed vets services act.com

S